TENDER ROSES
for TOUGH
CLIMATES

TENDER ROSES
for
TOUGH CLIMATES

Douglas Green

Illustrations by Vince Babak

CHAPTERS PUBLISHING, LTD., SHELBURNE, VERMONT 05482

Published by
Chapters Publishing Ltd.
2085 Shelburne Road
Shelburne, Vermont 05482

Library of Congress Cataloging-in-Publication Data
Green, Douglas.
    Tender roses for tough climates / Douglas Green.
        p.   cm.
    Includes bibliographical references and index.
    ISBN 1-57630-031-5 (hardcover). — ISBN 1-57630-032-3 (softcover)
    1. Rose culture—Snowbelt States. 2. Rose culture—Canada. 3. Roses.
    I. Title.
    SB411.G818   1997
    633.9'33734'097—dc21   96-51616

Printed and bound in the USA by
World Color Book Services

Designed by Susan McClellan

Cover: 'Charlotte Armstrong' hybrid tea rose; photograph by Saxon Holt
Title Page: 'Peace' hybrid tea rose; photograph by Derek Fell
Contents Page: 'Paradise' hybrid tea rose; photograph by Derek Fell

ACKNOWLEDGMENTS

IT SEEMS AS IF THIS ROSE BOOK STARTED A LONG WAY back in my gardening life, and, as with most things, there have been other people intimately involved along the way. While they don't get mentioned on the book spine, I think they deserve some of the credit for their actions. As the author, it falls to me to accept the praise for the book and the blame for any errors, but it is these people who have kept me on the straight and narrow.

The first is, of course, my wife, Andrea, who is directly responsible for the entire book. After all, it was her command, "Grow me those!" that got me growing roses in the first place. That bed of 'Tiffany' hybrid tea roses has been a never-ending source of family tales, and Andrea's place in the story should never be diminished.

I have to mention my children, Elizabeth, Robert, Jennifer and Christina, because they are firmly convinced that they do all the summer work around the nursery while I sit in my office and write. They may have a small point.

My agent, Susan Urstadt, who has encouraged me from start to finish. I send her a much deserved bouquet.

My aunt, Violet Matthews, whose garden has been my far north experimental test plot for the past 10 years. Her USDA Zone 3 garden grows many of the roses listed here. Aunt Vi also read the manuscript and passed along her comments, for which she receives my thanks and public recognition.

Barb Alguire also read the manuscript and passed along valuable comments from the perspective of one of the few gardeners I know who grows more vegetables than roses.

The folks at Chapters who decided to produce the book: Paul, who got stuck being my editor again and who continues to demand clarity; Susan, who has produced another magnificent piece of artwork called a book; and Barry, who stoically answers my calls and still says it's okay to call him. The unnamed talented folks who worry away the countless details—thank you.

CONTENTS

Roses like this 'Tiffany' hybrid tea
have long been symbols of
love and beauty.

INTRODUCTION

THERE IS AN EMOTION IN GARDENERS THAT
ignores hard logic. We see a beautiful flower
and we want it for our yard—never mind
that our climate may be unsuitable, that the
plant may die the first winter we set it out.
No plant, it seems, triggers this desire more than the rose. We
walk through a formal garden, or even glance through the
pages of a book, and see the deep tones and delicately folded
petals of the flowers. We inhale their perfumed scent and find
ourselves murmuring "I want."

My wife fell captive to this rose mystique some years ago
when we ventured 400 miles south from our Ontario farmstead
and nursery to tour the famous Longwood Gardens in Pennsylvania. When she saw an expanse of hybrid tea roses called
'Tiffany' and stooped to enjoy their rose-pink blossoms, she
was entranced by their floral charm.

"Grow me those," she said. And I wanted to oblige. As the
owner of a perennial plant nursery, Simple Gifts Farm, I
thought it would be easy. Many northern gardeners do. Unfortunately, they are often wrong, sadly so. No matter how they
mulch, hill and pamper their roses, the plants die in their in-
hospitably cold climate. Winter, the great leveler, casually
wreaks its vengeance on their garden dreams.

To succeed with our 'Tiffanies' I used an unusual planting
method that first came to my attention through an article in a
Canadian rose journal. I conducted my own field trials on

proper feeding and pruning. I experimented with different planting depths. And I learned that cold-tender roses could survive our frigid winter, without elaborate protection, if planted more deeply than in traditional rose culture. The "deep planting method" is described in the first two chapters of this book.

The days of failure are over. Gardeners in colder parts of the country can grow tender roses, confident their plants will endure the winter and radiantly bloom again in the spring. Keeping roses alive simply means changing the way we plant and grow them. What makes the deep planting method even more appealing is that rather than adding chores to the landscaping calendar, it saves work.

Some climbing roses, such as 'William Baffin', endure winter cold without coddling.

I confess to being a lazy gardener. With the size of our gardens, there isn't time to lavish a lot of winter care on needy plants. None of our roses get special treatment. There is no hilling, no wrapping, no insulating. A normal fall pruning and we wish our roses good night for their winter's nap.

In other respects, too, we have learned that roses are less demanding than many traditional gardening books suggest. They need not be magnets for every pest and plague and need not be doused endlessly with toxic powders and sprays. With good soil, adequate moisture and regular feeding, roses can thrive, largely free of insects and disease.

It took many years to achieve our system of keeping roses alive through our cold winters. Our patience has been rewarded. 'Tiffany' roses now perfume our gardens. 'Blaze' roses trail from hanging baskets, while 'William Baffin', 'John Cabot' and other hardy climbers grace trellises and walls. Our rose-growing hopes are now reality. This book explains chapter by chapter how you can realize the same dreams. However cold your winters, your summers can still be warm with roses.

Chapter One

ROSE CULTURE

N O OTHER ORNAMENTAL PLANT TRACES its roots as far back in time as the rose. A symbol of beauty and inspiration to artists and poets, the rose has been cultivated for at least 4,000 years. The cultivated roses of today are descended from more than 150 species of wild roses. Most of them are indigenous to Asia, but many are found throughout much of the world's northern temperate zones.

Cultivated roses can be grouped in five large categories, three of which are of particular interest to most gardeners: bush roses, climbing roses and shrub roses. The remaining categories include miniatures and tree roses, also of interest to many growers.

In the bush rose class are the modern hybrid teas with their large flowers and long stems, sporting familiar names such as 'Chrysler Imperial', 'Mister Lincoln' and 'Peace'. Floribundas are also bush

Beauty in profusion or singly: a lush array (above); 'Peace' rose (left).

*Clockwise from center back: 'Fantin-Latour', 'Ragged Robin' and 'Mary Rose'
are among the hundreds of shrub varieties for informal gardens.*

roses, but unlike hybrid teas, they bear clusters of medium-sized blossoms throughout the summer. 'Sarabande', 'Ma Perkins' and 'Fabergé' are among the popular floribunda varieties. Grandifloras are similar in flowering to floribundas in that they produce clusters of blossoms. The flowers can be larger than those on floribundas, closer to the size of hybrid teas, and the plants themselves are generally taller than floribundas. 'Queen Elizabeth' is a popular grandiflora variety, as are 'Camelot' and 'Carousel'.

Climbing roses have been bred to be repeat bloomers or everblooming types. Many climbers bear their blossoms in clusters like floribundas. Despite the proliferation of repeat-blossoming varieties, many gardeners remain enthusiastic about old-fashioned climbers that flower for only a brief period each summer but bear blossoms with captivating scents. 'John Cabot', 'Dortmund' and 'Jens Munk' are among the varieties that can be trained to climb.

Shrub roses can differ widely in size, depending on their type. Some can become great hulking bushes that almost defy pruning, while others grow 4 to 5 feet high and about as wide. The spreading nature of many shrub varieties makes them a wonderful choice in informal landscapes, where they can ramble with some abandon. Shrub roses include more than a dozen different rose types, such as bourbons, damasks and gallicas. 'Graham Thomas', 'Zéphirine Drouhin' and 'Fantin-Latour' are among the hundreds of shrub varieties.

WINTER HARDINESS

THOUGH ROSES HAVE BEEN grown for centuries in many parts of the world, they pose a particular challenge for gardeners north of USDA Zone 6, a demarcation line that runs through southern New York, Pennsylvania and Ohio, and westward. Many roses that gardeners are eager to grow, particularly the eye-catching hybrid teas, floribundas and grandifloras, and some climbing types, cannot endure the deep cold of northern winters.

Without elaborate winter protection — and sometimes even with protection — these tender types may bloom a season or two and then succumb to the cold. That, at least, is the discouraging scenario if you follow traditional rose-planting advice.

But it need not be. Experience has shown me that tender roses can survive intense cold with no winter protection, if they are planted properly. Following what I call the "deep planting method," I have kept dozens of hybrid teas alive through a decade of Canadian winters at our farm and plant nursery in

Climbing roses pose a particular challenge for gardeners north of USDA Zone 6.

Ontario (USDA Zone 4) without coddling them. And with the arrival of June, I have been able to enjoy the clouds of fragrance emanating from their blossoms and to cut elegant bouquets to grace the dining table.

Extensive experimentation has shown me that, for cold climates, the most successful strategy is to plant hybrid teas, floribundas, grandifloras and hardy climbing types so the graft, or bud union, is 6 inches below ground. The bud union is easy to recognize by the joint or swelling where the top of the bush is grafted to the roots. (Deep planting is described in detail in Chapter Two.)

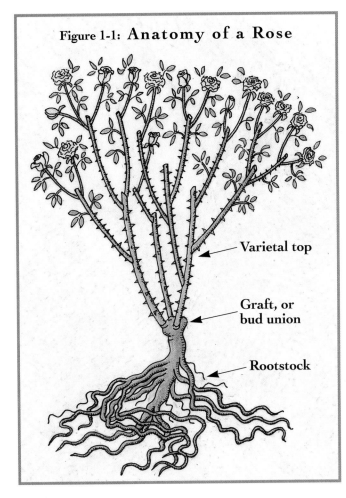

Figure 1-1: Anatomy of a Rose

Varietal top

Graft, or bud union

Rootstock

ROSE ANATOMY

To appreciate the value of the deep planting method, it is useful to understand something of rose anatomy. Hybrid roses—teas, floribundas, grandifloras and many other types—are grafted together from a rootstock that is cold-hardy and a top that may be quite sensitive to cold. The top carries the rose variety; the roots provide the sustenance (Figure 1-1). Grafting enables growers to produce thousands of genetically similar roses and get them ready for market in two years rather than the three years commonly needed for plants grown on their own roots.

In mild climates, the grafted partnership works beautifully. In England, where rose growing is a national passion and where much research and writing has been done, gardeners often set out plants with the graft, or bud union, at or just above the ground.

In a colder climate, the English planting style requires extensive winter protection, not to save the roots but to preserve the grafted top. Otherwise, the desirable flowering branches will be killed. Shoots may continue to grow from the roots, but these suckers will not produce the colorful flowers that the gardener expected.

HORTICULTURAL REQUIREMENTS

Tender roses require special attention for winter survival (as discussed in Chapter Two), but all roses benefit from optimum growing conditions.

Sunlight

The first prerequisite for elegant roses is plenty of sunshine. Without at least six hours of good, strong sunlight every day, roses will not have the reserves to produce beautiful flowers. Their canes will be thin and weak. Their susceptibility to disease will increase. Finally, their lack of vigor will leave them vulnerable to winter cold.

Figure 1-2 illustrates how much sunlight is needed for good roses. Roses grow best in areas B, C and E, or any combination of the three. By themselves, areas A, D and F do not generally offer enough sunlight.

Nevertheless, with some roses, it may be possible to achieve a measure of success in less-than-optimum sunlight. If a potential site

Figure 1-2: **What Is Sun, What Is Shade?**

The quality of sunlight a rose receives varies not only with the total length of exposure but with the time of day the light is received. An hour of morning sun is less intense than an hour at midday. The accompanying key describes six different exposures, or times, when a plant might receive sunlight and defines the value of each in terms of sun and shade. For example, if a rose receives direct sun only between 6 AM and 10 AM, it is said to be in a shady location and will not thrive.

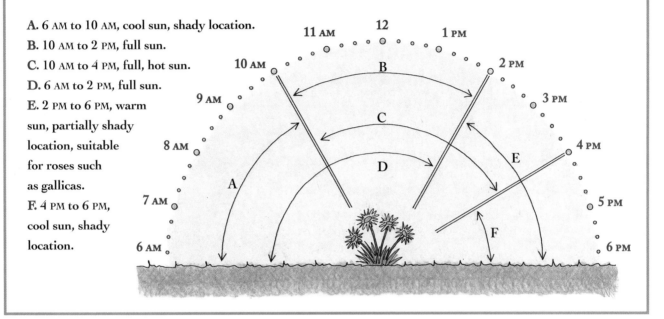

A. 6 AM to 10 AM, cool sun, shady location.
B. 10 AM to 2 PM, full sun.
C. 10 AM to 4 PM, full, hot sun.
D. 6 AM to 2 PM, full sun.
E. 2 PM to 6 PM, warm sun, partially shady location, suitable for roses such as gallicas.
F. 4 PM to 6 PM, cool sun, shady location.

has six hours of sunshine a day at the height of the season, gardeners may want to try a rosebush. Start with a single plant in the sunniest spot and expand the collection if the rose thrives. If the only sunny location is the patio, see Chapter Five for detailed instructions on container rose growing.

Good Soil

Roses will grow in a surprisingly wide range of soils, from heavy clay to light sand. However, the better the soil, the more vigorous the plant and the more prolific its flowers.

Even the poorest soil can be steadily improved with loosening and aerating, and with the addition of organic material. One soil preparation technique, called double-digging, can benefit every type of rose—indeed, every plant in the garden. It is particularly appropriate for roses grown with the deep planting method because their elaborate roots can easily spread into the loosened ground and feed on the rich organic matter worked into the subsoil.

Double-Digging

Double-digging involves turning and loosening the soil in a bed to a depth of 18 inches or so, about twice the length of a shovel blade. In the process, you can add amendments to enhance the fertility of the soil and improve its structure. Adding organic material will

Figure 1-3: **Double-Digging Technique**

Loosening the soil to a depth of two shovel blades can make a dramatic improvement in the quality of your roses.

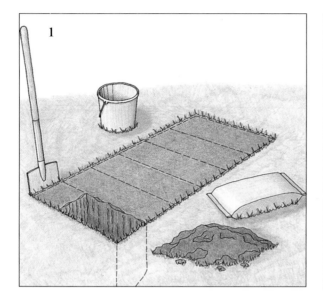

1. Excavate a trench about 1 foot wide and about two shovel blades deep across the end of the bed and leave the soil beside the bed or put it in a wheelbarrow.

2. Dig a second trench of the same dimensions as the first, and use the excavated soil from the second trench to fill in the first.

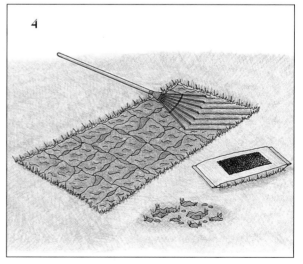

3. Continue trenching the length of the bed, adding soil amendments as you go. Collect any rocks, roots and weeds in a bucket.

4. Use the soil from the first trench to fill in the last one, then rake the bed smooth.

increase the moisture-holding capacity of sandy soil. And in heavy clay, organic matter will enhance drainage, allowing water and air to move more easily through the soil.

To begin, dig a trench approximately 1 foot wide and 18 inches deep across the width of the bed (Figure 1-3). Remove any rocks, weeds, roots and other unwanted material. Load the soil from the first trench into buckets or a wheelbarrow and move it to the far end of the bed.

Next, dig a second trench of the same width and depth right beside the first, shoveling the newly dug soil into the first trench. Proceed down the bed in this same manner, one trench at a time. As you fill in the first trench, you can add compost, well-rotted manure or peat moss. Our recipe is to mix two shovelfuls of amendments—one of composted manure and one of peat moss—with every three shovelfuls of garden soil, spread across the width of the bed. Repeat the "three shovels, two shovels" mantra as you proceed down the bed.

Phosphorus in the form of bone meal can also be added if you are digging the bed for the first time. One or two handfuls of bone meal for every six shovels of soil will put an adequate supply of phosphorus in the root zone of the roses.

Use what soil you need from the first trench to fill in the last one. Even though you are removing roots, weeds and stones, you are also adding amendments and loosening the ground, so the soil in the bed will be slightly higher than it was before you started. Rake the bed smooth after you finish digging. The soil will now have excellent aeration and good

fertility down to the root depth of roses that are deeply planted.

Rototilling is not a substitute for double-digging. A tiller works only the top 6 to 8 inches of soil, and it tends to create a dense, compact subsurface layer of hardpan that tender roots have trouble penetrating. Rototillers also cut roots into small pieces capable of sprouting new growth, suddenly multiplying the weed population a hundredfold.

Organic matter helps the growth and flowering of any rose. Spread compost around the plants every spring and very lightly cultivate it into the soil. Earthworms are great helpers in incorporating compost, but it may take a few years to build up a large worm population in your beds. One way to attract worms is to pile leaves 4 inches deep over the entire rose bed in the fall. By the following July, the worms will have begun their magic, reducing the thick pile of leaves to shreds. As the worm population grows, the improvement in soil health will be dramatic.

The natural soil of our nursery is a good sandy loam, but our old farmhouse is situated on the top of a rocky knoll with very shallow soil. Many loads of fill were needed to create our gardens, and most of it came from our township, when workers were cleaning out drainage ditches. The quality of our garden soil, then, is extremely variable and makes for a continuing experiment in what will grow in which conditions. Over time, we have learned that roses will grow in many different soil textures. However, the critical element is always the same: water. Roses need adequate moisture to thrive.

Roses and perennials form a colorful combination that extends garden bloom time.

Chapter One ❧ *Rose Culture*

Watering

Roses require less irrigation on clay soils than on sandy soils. This may be compensation to gardeners whose heavy soil is not well suited for many plants. Rather than struggle with perennials, the clay-based gardener can switch to roses and become the envy of the neighborhood. A range of species, from taller shrub roses to small hybrid teas, can flower and perfume the garden for the entire growing season.

To say that roses grow well in clay is not to suggest they are incompatible with sandy soil, however. Success in sandy soil is a matter of adding copious amounts of compost every spring and watering the roses attentively throughout the growing season. It is the lack of water that limits the success of roses in light soils. Provide water at the base of the plant, either through a weekly soaking of manure tea or through irrigation from a hose. Three gallons of water a week is a reasonable average per plant. Water needs will vary, of course, depending on the weather and the size and condition of the plant. A large shrub rose in full bloom will require more water than a small hybrid tea with only a few buds.

In heavy clay soil, divide a weekly watering into three 1-gallon portions. If the soil is still wet from one watering or from rain, wait a couple of days and check it again before irrigating.

In very sandy soils, which don't hold water for any length of time, it may be best to divide a 3-gallon weekly watering into two applications.

To judge whether the ground needs water, scrape away the top half-inch or so and feel if the soil is dry. Roses grow best in soil that is evenly moist but not spongy.

Fertilizing

Fertilizers are often categorized under two broad headings: macronutrients and micronutrients. Roses need macronutrients in larger quantities than micros, but both are essential for healthy plant growth. A tiny bit of copper may be just as important to a plant as a large amount of nitrogen. Put in automotive terms, you might say that a tiny spring in the fuel system is just as important as a tank full of gas. Without either one, the car will not run.

The macronutrients are nitrogen, phosphorus and potassium, and they are needed in relatively large quantities for roses to thrive and bloom. Among the important micronutrients needed for good growth are sulfur, calcium, magnesium, boron, molybdenum, iron, zinc, manganese and copper.

Compost, manure and seaweed are excellent sources of micronutrients. Compost and manure also build the soil, improving its fertility and water-holding capacity. Use them generously and your roses will respond with good growth and prolific blooms.

If you buy synthetic fertilizer at a garden center, it's useful to understand how the product is formulated. The primary plant foods in most fertilizers are the macronutrients: nitrogen, phosphorus and potassium. The amount of these constituents contained in any product is represented by a number displayed on the package. The formula always lists the nutrients in alphabetical order. A 10-10-10 fertilizer has 10 percent nitrogen, 10 percent phosphorus and 10 percent potassium. The

*Feeding the soil stimulates lush growth
and large flowers.*

rest of the product is composed of inert ingredients.

Nutrients work in combination, together contributing to the general vigor of a plant. To assign specific influence to individual nutrients is something of an oversimplification. However, it may be useful as a broad guideline. For example, nitrogen is particularly important in stimulating lush foliage and top growth. Phosphorus promotes root and stem development. And potassium contributes to flowering and fruiting and overall health.

Different fertilizers are formulated for different plants. For example, a turf fertilizer, which is high in nitrogen, would not be applicable for roses. If you applied it at the recommended rate, it might burn the plants. Yet if you reduced the amount, the roses

might be starved for other nutrients.

Products sold specifically for roses are not absolutely necessary, but it is important to use a roughly balanced formula in which the percentages of macronutrients are identical or similar, such as a 10-10-10 or a 9-12-7.

The amount of fertilizer a rose needs depends on the analysis of the product and a test of the soil. Bagged manure typically has an analysis of 1-1-1, while a common synthetic fertilizer would have a 10-10-10 analysis. Since the numbers refer to the percentages of each constituent, 100 pounds of manure would contain 1 pound of nitrogen, the same amount found in 10 pounds of a 10-10-10 product.

Here is a formula for determining the number of pounds of a fertilizer to apply when you know how much of a macronutrient you need per 100 square feet:

$$\frac{100}{\substack{\text{the percentage} \\ \text{of the nutrient} \\ \text{in the fertilizer}}} \quad \mathbf{X} \quad \substack{\text{the pounds} \\ \text{of nutrient} \\ \text{needed per} \\ \text{100 square feet}}$$

Let's say that, based on a soil test, you want to put on 1 pound of nitrogen per 100 square feet. You would divide the number of square feet—100—by the percentage of nitrogen in the fertilizer—say, 10 percent—and multiply the answer—10—by the amount of nitrogen needed, in this case, 1 pound. The recommended application rate, then, would be 10 pounds of fertilizer over the 100-square-foot area. If you use manure with a 1-1-1 analysis, you would need 100 pounds.

The fertilizer needs of a garden can be accurately determined only with a soil test conducted by a reputable laboratory. Many cooperative extension service labs offer a thorough test of nutrient levels for less than $20. Without a soil test, adding fertilizer is a guessing game, at best. If your application rate is too low, the plants will not perform well. If it is too high, the plants may be burned or killed.

A lab test can also gauge the pH of the soil, indicating its relative acidity or alkalinity. A pH reading of 7.0 is neutral. Readings below 7.0 indicate acid soil; readings above 7.0 indicate alkaline conditions. Roses do best in slightly acid soil with a pH range of 6.2 to 6.8. The pH level can be modified to make an alkaline soil more suitable for roses. Adding sulfur, or, preferably, acidic organic matter such as peat moss, finely ground pine bark or oak leaf mold will lower soil pH. Excessively acid soil can be improved, or "sweetened," by adding dolomitic limestone.

Manure and Compost Teas and Liquid Fish Fertilizer

Fertilizing teas have an important place in rose culture, both in traditional practice and in the deep planting method. The teas have a pungent odor, but their effect on plants is certainly appealing to the eye. Leaves become a lush green. Shoots develop lovely reddish tones and reach for the sky in their haste to give forth flowers, which open large and full.

Brewing a fertilizing tea is easy. You can fill a burlap sack with three or four shovelfuls of manure or compost and steep it in 5 gallons of water. Leave the sack in the pail until the water turns a deep brown. You can keep using the manure until it stops coloring the water. Three to four shovelfuls of manure is enough to brew 30 to 40 gallons of tea. When the "tea bag" stops brewing brown liquid, you can spread the contents on the garden to build up the organic level of the soil.

Once a week, pour about 3 gallons of tea around the roots of each plant. To discourage the spread of disease, make an effort to avoid wetting the foliage.

If manure or compost is not readily available or making tea is too much of a chore, you can buy a liquid fish fertilizer and apply it according to the package instructions. Fish emulsion is an excellent source of micronutrients.

Experiments in our garden have consistently shown that roses thrive on manure tea. Even though we add generous amounts of composted manure to the soil every fall, we have found that giving the plants a weekly serving of manure tea, and thereby watering them deeply, is an important contribution to first-class blooms.

The importance of liquid feeding cannot be overemphasized in the northern planting system. Rose roots grow so deeply that frequent fertilizing with manure tea or fish emulsion is essential for getting nutrients down to the hungry feeder roots.

MULCHES

MULCHES BENEFIT THE GARDEN and the gardener in so many ways that it is difficult to imagine horticulture without them. First of all, mulches reduce weeding. A government study not long ago found that a 4-inch layer of mulch cut weeding by more than 90 percent. The study also found that reducing the depth of the mulch increased the number of weeds that had to be eliminated by hand. Government studies often confirm what we already know. With mulches, deeper is better.

Mulches also conserve water. Spreading a few inches of organic matter over the soil will markedly reduce evaporation by sun and wind. If gardeners want to cut their water bill, mulching will help.

Organic matter moderates sudden changes in soil temperature. Soil under an organic mulch is less likely to constantly freeze and thaw in fluctuating winter temperatures and is less likely to become exceedingly hot under a punishing summer sun. Mulched ground is also slower to heat up in the spring and slower to cool down in the fall. In fact, because mulch slows soil warming in the spring, you may want to pull it away from the base of your roses as the ground thaws and rake it back when the canes begin to grow.

Mulches also discourage many insects. Pests such as earwigs love to dine on decaying organic matter, so they tend to feed on the lower layers of mulch, leaving your roses alone.

Almost any organic material will serve as a mulch. Ideally, it should be inexpensive, readily available and stay in place in the garden. Straw, grass clippings and chopped leaves make excellent mulches. Bark chips, chopped cedar and cocoa bean hulls are also often used. One organic material that is not a good choice is peat moss: If peat moss dries out, it forms an impervious layer on the soil and prevents water from percolating down to the plant's root zone.

In the rose garden, you may want to choose a mulch as much for its visual appeal as for its other functions. Big chunks of dark-colored bark lend a formal appearance to the beds, while light-colored and finely shredded materials tend to have a more informal look. Regardless of your choice, adding an inch or so of fresh mulch at the end of the growing season will enhance the appearance of the garden.

MICROCLIMATES

EVEN IN A SMALL GARDEN, NOT ALL areas share the exact climatological conditions. Different exposures to wind and sun and proximity to large thermal masses can create varying climatic zones. Taking advantage of favorable microclimates can further protect tender roses.

Plant roses out of the reach of prevailing winds. Or put in evergreen hedges or fences as windbreaks. Full summer sun ensures rose blooms, but full winter sun promotes survival. Sheltering a bush from winter winds and giving it the benefit of sun creates a microclimate that can be surprisingly milder than more shaded areas just a few feet away.

Heat from thermal masses (such as buildings, boulders or concrete) radiates into the soil and helps keep tender roots alive during colder winters. Planting near a south-facing foundation is one way rosebushes can benefit from solar gain.

Avoid low-lying areas for rose planting.

As foundation plantings, roses are a charming alternative to evergreens. Being close to a building gives the plants some protection from winter cold.

Cool air is heavier than warm air and, like water, collects in low spots. Dips and valleys will receive earlier fall frost and later frost in the spring than upland gardens. Airflow is similar to the movement of water. If there are places in the garden where water will collect, cool air will collect there, too.

Hedges and fences at the base of a slope will trap cool air. At the top of a rise, they may offer warmth by diverting breezes away from the plants behind them. If there are places where water will create cool eddies, such as around trees, be assured that flowing air will do the same. Understanding some of these subtleties will enable you to chart air movement through your gardens and identify warmer microclimates. Taking advantage of a favorable microclimate can be akin to moving your rose garden 100 miles to the south.

With prudent site selection and care, northern gardeners can find delight in a whole range of roses. Even tender hybrid teas can survive year after year, gracing the garden with their large, delicately shaped flowers.

Chapter Two

TENDER ROSES

T HE LARGE-FLOWERING HYBRID TEA ROSES, floribundas and grandifloras—those showy blossoms that fill the summer landscape with perfumed scents—can prove elusive to northern gardeners. They are not well adapted to survive the rigors of a long, cold winter. Commonly, in gardens north of USDA Zone 6, these tender roses require elaborate protection to give them any chance of living through the cold season. Even with protection, they may bloom for only a few years before dying in a particularly severe cold spell.

Happily, that frigid fate can be avoided. Tender roses can survive the cold, and with no winter protection. The secret to keeping them alive and thriving is to plant the bushes more deeply than in traditional rose culture. If the graft, or bud union, on the plant is set 6 inches below ground, enough of the cold-tender top will survive

Hybrid teas (above and left) are jewels in the crown of a summer morning.

The legginess of some hybrid teas is artfully disguised by interplanting them with perennials.

to vigorously emerge again in the spring. The bud union is easy to recognize by the joint or swelling on the stem where the top of the bush is grafted to the roots (see Figure 1-1, page 18).

Deep planting may sound heretical to some experienced rose growers. Conventional wisdom has always held that the bud union should be at the soil level or, at most, 2 inches below ground. This might be fine in England and milder parts of the United States, but it is definitely not deep enough to ensure survival in colder areas, such as our USDA Zone 4 gardens, without the chore of added winter protection. With deep planting,

the canes are permanently protected in the earth and insulated with almost a half-foot of soil.

In traditional rose culture, the most common winter protection method has always been "hilling," which involves building a 12- to 18-inch mound of soil over the rose canes in the fall. In the spring, the mound is raked away to expose the canes and nascent buds to the warmth of the sun. Wood chips, straw, thermal blankets, peat moss or commercially made rose cones are also used for hilling.

In spite of this annual effort, roses still die, which is why I began experimenting in search of a better method. I have tried putting the bud union at various depths from 4 to about 12 inches, and found that the 6-inch depth is the perfect compromise between winter survival and prolific summer flowering. A greater depth might allow bushes to grow in climates colder than our USDA Zone 4 nursery, but the roots would be so deep that you would need an extremely generous, frequent feeding regimen to keep the bushes flowering.

Deep planting has been greeted with skepticism by some experienced rosarians. They raise questions about the survival of aboveground canes, about the proliferation of root suckers and about delayed blooming.

Many years of trials have shown me that these concerns are not valid. It is true that aboveground canes will not survive. But I don't leave any canes above ground. In the fall, I prune them to ground level. In the spring, new growth emerges from the remaining canes below ground.

As far as root suckers are concerned, I have been experimenting with deep planting for 10 years, and with hybrid teas, floribundas and grandifloras, I have yet to see my first unwanted shoots.

Deeply planted roses may produce their first blooms later in the spring than roses that have been hilled for the winter, but like traditionally planted bushes, ours still produce three flushes of flowers during the season. Sometimes the last blooms appear slightly later in the fall.

PLANTING PREPARATION

AS IN TRADITIONAL ROSE CULTURE, the width of the hole for a deeply planted rose should be about twice the diameter of the root ball, so that the feeder roots can grow into loose, aerated soil. The depth of the hole, of course, needs to be greater than in traditional practice. To ensure proper depth, you may want to measure the rosebush

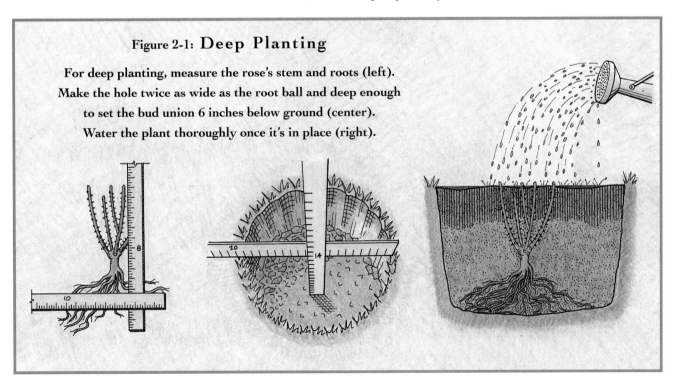

Figure 2-1: **Deep Planting**

For deep planting, measure the rose's stem and roots (left).
Make the hole twice as wide as the root ball and deep enough
to set the bud union 6 inches below ground (center).
Water the plant thoroughly once it's in place (right).

Fragrant flowers of the hybrid tea 'Charlotte Armstrong' can open to 5 inches.

from the bud union to the root tips (if it is a bare-root plant) or to the bottom of its container (if it is container-grown), then add 6 inches to allow for the distance the bud union should be below ground. Once you know how deep the hole should be dug, you can check your progress by setting a stick across the top of the hole and measuring down to gauge the hole's depth (see Figure 2-1, page 31). Soil preparation, as described in the discussion on double-digging in Chapter One, pages 19-21, is important to the establishment of any rose.

Before you set the rose in its hole, examine its top and, if it is a bare-root specimen, its roots. Prune off any broken roots. Also prune any damaged canes back to fat, healthy-looking buds. If the plant is in poor condition—perhaps a hand-me-down from a friend's garden or the only available specimen of some desired variety—the few viable buds may be far down on the canes, near the bud union. Perhaps pruning back to this good wood will leave only a few inches of cane, but go ahead and make the cuts. Without drastic pruning, the tops may continue to die back, eventually killing the entire cane.

PLANTING DORMANT AND IN-LEAF ROSES

IF YOU ARE PLANTING A DORMANT ROSE-bush, one with no leaves and no swollen buds on its canes, you can set it in its hole with the bud union 6 inches deep and fill in

Figure 2-2: **Planting an In-Leaf Rose**

When planting an in-leaf rose, fill the hole only to the level of the graft, as shown. After the rose is dormant, fill the hole so the graft is 6 inches below ground.

around its top with enriched soil. Dormant buds can be buried without injury. When they begin to grow, they will become young shoots emerging from the ground to form strong new canes.

If the rose is already in leaf or its buds are swelling, you can still plant the bush at the proper depth, but you cannot completely fill in the hole until the end of the season, when the canes are dormant (Figure 2-2). Burying leaves and emerging buds can quickly kill a plant. My approach with leafed-out roses is to fill the hole only to the level of the bud union. Let the rose grow until the end of the season, then finish filling in the trench in the fall when the plant is dormant.

As an alternative, you can plant the rose in a shallower hole and enjoy it all summer. When it becomes dormant, dig it up and replant it with the bud union 6 inches deep to ensure its winter survival.

A third option is to grow the rose in its pot all summer, then plant it in the fall. (See Chapter Five, pages 84-99, for detailed instructions on caring for container roses.)

PLANTING BARE-ROOT AND CONTAINER-GROWN ROSES

ROSES ARE USUALLY SHIPPED OR SOLD in one of three different ways: They may be bare-root, they may be in a plastic pot or they may be in a fiber container. Any of these arrangements can produce beautiful roses, but each must be handled differently when you are preparing the rose for planting (Figure 2-3).

Bare-Root Stock

Bare-root roses, those sold with no soil around their roots, are common in the mail-order trade because they are light and relatively inexpensive to ship. The roses are dug from the producer's fields in the fall and either sent directly to gardeners or garden centers or kept in cold storage and shipped in the spring.

Some authorities recommend that before you plant a bare-root rose, you soak it in a pail of water for a few hours to rehydrate its roots. While this is not bad advice, the practice seems unnecessary. I have found no difference in vitality and longevity between bare-root roses that have been soaked before planting and those that I have not soaked but have heavily watered or "puddled in" after planting.

If you decide to soak bare-root plants, don't leave them in water overnight, or they may drown for lack of oxygen. Two to three hours is plenty of time to wet the roots.

Whether the rose is soaked or not, never allow the roots to dry out. Keep plants in the

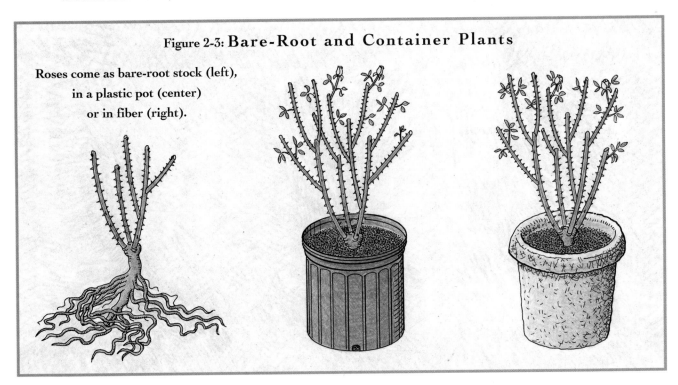

Figure 2-3: **Bare-Root and Container Plants**

Roses come as bare-root stock (left), in a plastic pot (center) or in fiber (right).

The 'Mary Rose' is an English shrub rose widely admired for the wonderful
fragrance and intricate shape of its flowers.

shade, wrapped in a damp cloth, until they are ready to be set out. If they dry out, even for few minutes, the delicate feeder roots will be damaged. I take more care with roses than almost any other plant in our nursery to ensure that the roots are continuously damp.

Another popular but equally unnecessary bit of advice regarding bare-root roses is that the roots be spread over a cone-shaped mound of soil at the bottom of the planting hole. No rose that was planted in our gardens was amenable to spreading its roots in any specific shape, never mind uniformly over a cone of soil.

Bare-root roses go into the ground in whatever contorted shape they arrive at our gardens. Simply make the hole large enough so that no roots are bent or forced in unnatural directions. Fit the hole to the plant, not the plant to the hole.

Plastic Pots

A rose that's sold in a plastic pot from a reputable nursery usually means that the plant has been in the pot for at least 12 months. It is common nursery practice to put up bare-root stock in plastic containers and keep it for about a year before selling it, at

Carefully remove a rose from its plastic pot, keeping the root ball intact.
If the plant is stuck, soaking the soil will make it easier to slide out.

which point the plant is referred to as container-grown stock. This potting up and holding process gives the roots plenty of time to become established in the planting medium, which means there should be very little transplant shock when the rose is set out.

Make the planting hole about twice as wide as the pot so the rose's feeder roots can grow into loosened, aerated soil. Carefully remove the rose from the pot to keep its root ball intact, and ease it into the planting hole at the appropriate depth. If the rose is difficult to remove from the pot, tip it upside down and pull up on the pot while tugging

down on the stem of the rose. Soaking the soil until water runs out the bottom of the pot will also help loosen the plant. Then fill the hole with soil and soak it until the surface is puddled.

Unfortunately, transplanting from a plastic pot is not always a smooth operation. The rose may have been in the pot for only a few months or weeks, giving the roots little time to become established. (The more responsible nursery practice, if the roses are going to be sold shortly after they are potted up, is to use fiber containers.)

If, when you remove the rose from its container, the soil falls away and you are left with a bare-root plant, there are a few techniques you can follow to minimize transplant shock. Set the rose in the ground as soon as possible and water it thoroughly. If the plant is leafed out, spray the foliage with a waxy substance called an antidesiccant to reduce moisture loss through the leaves. You may also want to complain to the garden center that the rose was not container-grown and ask for reimbursement if it dies.

A second possible problem with container-grown roses is, in a sense, the opposite of the first. The rose may have been in the container too long and may be pot-bound, with a tangle of roots completely encircling the container. This is not a difficult problem to solve. Separate out a few of the larger roots or make several vertical slices with a knife down the sides of the root mass. Cutting a few of the smaller roots will "wake up" the plant, which will send out vibrant new replacement roots into the surrounding soil.

Fiber Containers

Roses from garden centers are often sold in fiber pots. Garden centers purchase bare-root roses from large growers and pot them up a month or two before offering them for sale. Gardeners have to be careful with these fiber container roses, because their root development is just beginning. Upsetting this tender growth can slow the plant's establishment and subsequent flowering. Roses in fiber containers, however, are very easy to transplant, because they don't need to be removed from the pot.

Once the planting site is prepared, cut off the bottom of the fiber container so the roots can grow out into the moist soil. Next, set the pot in the hole. Lay a stick across the top of the hole and measure down from the stick to ensure that the bud union is at the proper depth.

If the rose is partially leafed out, it cannot be planted deeply until it goes dormant in the fall. At a shallower planting depth, the rim of the container may protrude above the ground. If it does—and this applies when setting out any plant in a fiber pot—break off the rim so the top will be covered with soil when the hole is filled. Otherwise, the rim may act as a wick and draw moisture from the sides of the pot and from the soil around the roots. If the sides are dry, the fiber material will not break down very quickly and will impede small feeder roots from working out of the container and into the surrounding soil.

After you set the pot in the hole, make a half-dozen vertical slices in the sides. This will enable water to move through, carrying bacteria that will help degrade the pot. In a short time, the roots will be established and the rose will be on its way to blooming.

FEEDING

TRADITIONALLY, ROSES ARE FED A chemical fertilizer in the spring to wake them up, and then fed again when they start to bloom. Late summer or fall feeding is not recommended, as the new shoots developed by this feeding are prone to winter damage.

In the deep planting system, a different approach is called for because the roots are so deep in the soil. Feeding is an ongoing task throughout the spring, summer and fall.

Long-stemmed hybrid teas, such as 'Oregold', make elegant bouquets.

After an initial generous spring feeding of compost or a helping of balanced rose food, provide weekly feedings of manure tea or fish emulsion. Begin these feedings when the first buds appear and continue them until the arrival of heavy frost. Liquid feeding not only supplies the roses with continual nutrition but provides water as well. Given this attentive care, the roses will bloom until the onset of freezing weather. (For more detailed feeding instructions, see the discussion on fertilizers and manure teas in Chapter One, pages 23-25.)

Having described this feeding regimen, I might add that gardens are not supposed to burden us with impossible demands. If you can't accommodate a weekly feeding program for all your roses, well, you can't. The plants will still provide a great deal of pleasure. The flowers may not be as large or as numerous, but they *will* smell as sweet.

PRUNING

THERE ARE VARIOUS TIMES DURING the year when it is necessary to prune deeply planted hybrid teas, floribundas and grandifloras. In late fall, after the plant has gone dormant and shed its leaves, cut the aboveground canes back to the soil line (Figure 2-4). Cutting them in the fall removes host material for overwintering disease organisms. And it takes care of a chore that you would otherwise face in the spring, because the aboveground canes would not survive the winter. As part of the pruning job, rake up any leaves from around each bush. Leaves, too, provide overwintering sites for disease and insect pests. A late-season pruning and neatening is consistent with the gardening adage that you should leave the garden in the fall as you would like to find it in the spring.

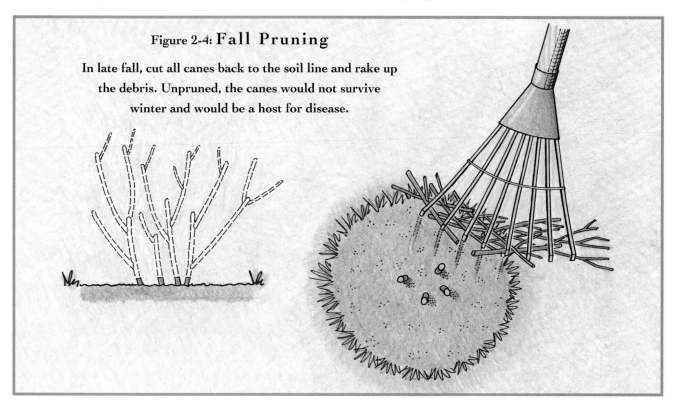

Figure 2-4: **Fall Pruning**

In late fall, cut all canes back to the soil line and rake up the debris. Unpruned, the canes would not survive winter and would be a host for disease.

Cutting canes back to the ground might seem alarming or aesthetically offensive to traditional rosarians, who welcome the appearance of green canes early in the spring. In traditional rose culture, canes are trimmed in the fall to a length of 12 to 18 inches. Soil is mounded up around them and removed early in the spring, allowing the buds to emerge on the surviving canes.

Hilling, however, is a lot of work and of limited success in our Zone 4 gardens. If you do hill your roses, be sure to import the soil from another part of the garden rather than from around your plants, which might insulate the tops but leave the roots exposed and vulnerable to the cold.

Summer pruning on the northern system is not greatly different from the traditional approach. The objective is twofold: to take off fading or dying flowers, and to encourage new, properly oriented growth. Removing spent flowers, or deadheading, improves the appearance of the plant, discourages disease and encourages more blossoms. Faded blooms are unsightly, littering the plant and the ground with decaying petals. The spent flowers are also hosts to fungal diseases and food for pests such as earwigs. Cutting each bloom when it begins to fade is a good house-keeping policy.

How far back do you cut each blossom and where do you make the cut? In northern gardens, roses produce more blooms if each spent blossom is pruned with a long stem. Removing 12 to 14 inches of stem encourages more shoots from the base of the plant and encourages more buds to grow into flowering branches. More shoots equal more flowers

Figure 2-5: Summer Pruning

Removing 12 to 14 inches of stem encourages basal shoots that will grow into flowering branches. Make each cut about ¼ inch above an outside-facing bud.

later in the season, when the plant blooms a second and third time.

Make each pruning cut about ¼ inch above an outside-facing bud (Figure 2-5). This bud will produce a new shoot that will grow away from the center of the plant and so keep the interior open, allowing better airflow and discouraging disease. Summer pruning becomes the art of finding and pruning back to these outside buds. If you must decide whether to remove a long piece of stem or to prune to an outside-facing bud, choose the outside bud, even if this means taking off only

This combination of the pink 'Nathalie Nypels', the red 'Mme. Norbert Levavasseur'
and the white 'Frau Karl Druschki' is as enduring as it is eye-catching.

4 or 5 inches of stem. Slightly slant all pruning cuts across the cane.

Plants are very resilient, so don't feel intimidated by the possibility of making an inappropriate cut. It may help to think that in the traditional rose-growing approach, northern gardeners generally only had one season to prune, or misprune, each rose before it died. Deep planting gives northern gardeners many years to experiment on the same plant.

Though I provide no winter care, deeply planted roses continue to thrive in the gardens surrounding our rural home. They accept this benign neglect as easily as the hardier perennials and woody plants that compete with them for space. I can enjoy their blooms all summer and confidently welcome winter knowing that the tender roses will return in the spring with their delightful colors and charming fragrance.

Chapter Three

CLIMBING ROSES

M OST CLIMBING ROSES ONLY VISIT northern gardens. I use the word "visit" because the plants rarely survive long and then only if a gardener provides attentive care. Generally, climbing roses must be untied from their trellis every fall and the canes bundled together with twine, wrapped with burlap or thermal blankets and buried in a trench. Once the rose is covered for the winter, rosarians have to wait hopefully for the next six months to find out whether their efforts were rewarded and the plant survived.

Fortunately, advances in rose breeding have freed northern gardeners from much of that labor and anxiety. A hardy breed of climbers has been developed at the Central Experimental Farm in Ottawa, Canada, by the botanist Felicitas Svejda. The roses are part of what is called the Explorer series, named for European voyagers

'Alexander Girault' (above) and 'Joseph's Coat' (left) require special care to overwinter.

EXPLORER SERIES ROSES

NAME	FLOWER COLOR	BOUQUET	GROWTH HABIT
Capt. Samuel Holland	Soft red, repeat blooming	Fragrant	Vigorous upright, pillar type; mildew and black spot resistant
David Thompson	Cyclamen-red, double	Very fragrant	Vigorous, upright; black spot and mildew resistant
Jens Munk	Lavender-pink, large double	Very fragrant	Upright, rugosa type, needs a lot of pruning to encourage climbing; mildew and black spot resistant
John Cabot	Medium red, double	Fragrant	Vigorous, upright; black spot and mildew resistant
Martin Frobisher	Light pink, double	Fragrant	Taller grower; black spot and mildew resistant
William Baffin	Deep pink, double, continuous blooms	Slightly fragrant	Vigorous, tall canes, glossy foliage; mildew resistant

who explored parts of Canada.

The Explorer types range in flowering and growth habit from the relatively compact 'Champlain', which blooms three times during the season, to the rangy 'John Cabot', which puts forth one magnificent floral display followed by smaller displays throughout the rest of the summer. Above is a description of what I consider the best and most widely available varieties in the Explorer series.

CREATIVE OPTIONS

Planting Explorer roses and coddling more tender varieties are not the only options northern gardeners have for raising climbers. With creative pruning and training, a hardy shrub-type multiflora or rugosa rose can be encouraged to grow along a fence or up a wall. It takes stout leather gloves and sharp pruners and a willingness to experiment, but northern growers can achieve beautiful displays with unusual species.

Gardeners in milder climates who can grow any number of tender, everblooming climbing varieties may disdain the hardy shrub types, with their brief flowering period. Northern gardeners, with fewer choices, need to be more creative in their horticulture practices and explore all the climbing possibilities. Later in this chapter you'll find detailed instruction on training hardy roses to climb.

A trellis of rough wood complements the unpretentious beauty of a 'William Baffin'.

Chapter Three ❧ *Climbing Roses*

'John Cabot' (above) and other climbers in the Explorer series have been bred for cold hardiness.

Chapter Three ❧ *Climbing Roses*

PLANTING CLIMBING ROSES

CLIMBING ROSES ARE SLIGHTLY EASIER to plant than hybrid teas and other tender, upright, bush types. The bud union of hardy climbing roses needs to be planted only about 2 inches deep, compared with the 6 inches for tender hybrids. The hardy climber will survive at the shallower depth and will not send out the unwanted extra shoots that sometimes emerge from deeply planted bushes of this type.

If you choose to grow tender climbing varieties, plant them with their bud union at or slightly above the soil line; deep planting is unnecessary because in the fall they will need to be dug up and the tops buried to protect the canes and flowering buds from freezing. Left on the trellis, tender climbing roses will not survive a severe winter.

There is one exception to these planting guidelines. If you want to train an Explorer-type rose as a spreading bush—for a garden centerpiece rather than as a climber—plant it with the bud union 6 inches deep. Over a few seasons, the buried canes will develop their own roots, and shoots will emerge each spring from these newly rooted canes. For a climbing rose, all this additional growth would not be desirable and would have to be pruned out each year. But the bounty of young canes will contribute fullness to a centerpiece planting, adding foliage as well as attractive flowers.

For a description of how to plant roses from different types of containers, see Chapter Two, pages 31-37.

CARE AND FEEDING

THE CARE OF CLIMBING ROSES IS similar to that of other hybrid types. Climbing roses need regular watering, adequate nutrition and proper pruning. However, in contrast to the care of deeply planted hybrids, climbers should not be fertilized or watered with manure tea after mid-July. Plants fertilized in late summer are apt to send out new, succulent growth that may be killed by winter cold.

Spent blossoms should be pruned off to remove a breeding ground for insects and disease. Deadheading also contributes to the appearance of the plant and encourages it to set more flowers. With each blossom, cut the stems back 12 to 14 inches to just above an out-facing bud.

WINTERING HARDY CLIMBERS

THE JOY OF HARDY CLIMBERS IS THAT they do not require any laborious preparations for winter. Perhaps the most important job is to remove the fallen leaves from around the base of the plant. Cleaning up the foliage takes away an overwintering site for the fungal disease black spot. Some roses, such as the Explorer 'Martin Frobisher', have resistance to black spot but are not immune to it. Any help you can give your plants by improving their environment will lessen the likelihood of disease. In other respects, the Explorers, like the intrepid souls they were named after, are a rugged lot and will take care of themselves as the cold season descends.

Figure 3-1: **Training and Pruning Hardy Climbing Roses**

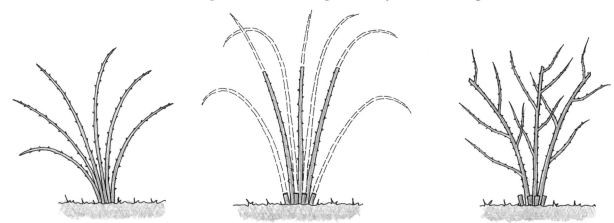

Allow the plant to grow unpruned and unsupported in its first year (above left). In the spring of
the second year, prune out all but three to five of the strongest canes. Remove about 6 inches from
the tips of these (above center). Tie the canes to a support or weave the tips through a trellis.
Side shoots will emerge from these canes (above right).

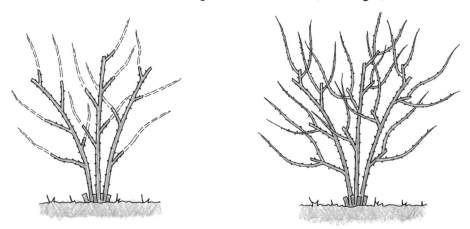

In the spring of the third year, cut back the side shoots, or laterals, by half their length (above left).
The rose will then develop strong new flower-bearing laterals (above right). In the fourth,
fifth and subsequent springs, remove one-third of the flowering canes and
cut back another third to 12 inches (below).

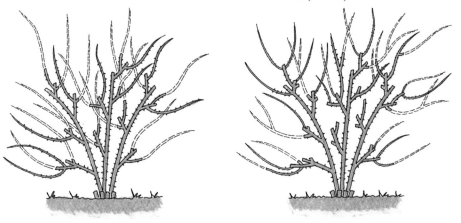

PRUNING THE HARDY CLIMBER

STRUCTURAL PRUNING IS BEST UNDER-
taken as winter gives way to spring.
There is no sense removing canes before the
damage of winter cold has been assessed.
Early spring pruning allows all the branches
the chance to live through the winter and
gives the gardener the most options for shaping and training the plant. My experience has
been that most of the Explorer series will be
fine every winter except for the winter that
comes on suddenly, before the newer, tender
canes have hardened off. Even then, damage
will be limited to a few canes that can be
pruned off to make way for the rush of spring
growth.

Hardy roses do not twine or cling to a trellis like climbing vines; they must be tied to the
uprights. I recommend using material that is
soft and will not cut into the canes, and in a
color that blends with the tones of the plant,
such as baling twine or green string. I also
suggest a tying method and material that is
easy to remove. It never seems to matter how
I tie the plant initially; I always want to
rearrange the pattern of the canes or change
their angle on the trellis. If the ties are quick
to cut, the work is faster and easier on the
hands.

Once the rose is established on a trellis, the
gardener's job is to keep the plant strong,
healthy and productive. By pruning systemat-
ically, you avoid having to take on an overgrown, unruly plant. Except for removing
spent flowers, all pruning is best done in the
early spring, before the plant breaks dormancy.

The object of ongoing pruning is to promote the growth of flowering shoots. Hardy
climbers bear most heavily on one-year-old
wood or on canes produced in the current
year. In general, prune out small, spindly
canes first (Figure 3-1). They will not produce good blossoms and by removing them,
you'll open up the rose, allowing better canes
to grow. The time spent thinning and shaping
your climbing rose will be rewarded with vigorous growth and prolific blooms.

WINTERING TENDER CLIMBERS

TENDER CLIMBING ROSES HAVE THEIR
enthusiastic fans, even among northern
gardeners, because they are long blooming
and offer desirable fragrances and colors—
especially yellows—not found on the hardier
species. However, keeping tender varieties
alive through a northern winter is not only
time consuming but chancy. An approach I
learned from a fellow nurseryman, who (unlike me) enjoys working with tender climbers,
is to bury each rose at least 8 to 12 inches
deep in the fall. The method works quite well,
and the nurseryman admits to losing plants to
only unusually harsh winters.

The seasonal preparation starts once the
leaves have fallen and the plant is dormant,
but the job has to be finished before the
ground freezes. In our Zone 4 climate, the
work is best undertaken toward the end of
October or very early in November, in part so
that most mice will have already found their
winter accommodations and be unlikely to
move into the rose trench and feed on the ten-

Pruning climbers is best done in early spring while the plants are dormant.
Trained to posts and beams, climbing roses can frame a structure in vibrant color.

der outer layers of the stems.

Remove the rose from its supports. Then dig the plant up, saving as many roots as you can. Force all the canes toward the center of the plant and bind them securely with stout twine. The objective in bundling is to make a tight package so that you can bury the plant in as small a trench as possible. Work with the natural shape of the plant; do not force the roots or canes and risk breaking the wood. Some gardeners wrap their bundled roses with burlap or flexible plastic foam, but this probably adds little to the protection provided by burying them at the recommended depth.

Dig a trench as long as the rose and deep enough to bury it at least 8 to 12 inches. Often a tight rose bundle will be about 12 inches thick and will require a trench 20 to 24 inches deep, which means enough digging to test most rosarians' commitment to tender climbers (Figure 3-2).

Before filling the trench, liberally sprinkle water-resistant mouse bait, carried in most hardware stores, inside the hole, or put the bait in a rubber boot tucked into the rose bundle near the roots. This will eliminate damage in case a few mice, making last-minute preparations for the winter season,

Figure 3-2: **Burying a Tender Climbing Rose**

After the plant is dormant, dig it up and remove it from its trellis (left). Bundle the bush with twine to form a tight column and lay it in a trench 20 to 24 inches deep. Sprinkle mouse bait over the canes and into a boot placed at the roots (below).

Fill in the trench (below left) and cover the area with 2 feet of leaves for added insulation (below right).

happen to come across the buried bush.

After filling in the trench, mound 2 feet of leaves over the whole area as further winter insulation.

As soon as winter has passed and the ground has thawed, dig up the rose and prune off any damaged canes. Replant it, water it and tie it to its trellis. If your efforts have been successful, buds will begin to swell as the weather warms. If not, hardy roses will seem a very attractive option.

CREATIVE TRAINING AND PRUNING

BECAUSE A ROSE IS CALLED A CLIMBER does not mean that it must grace only a wall or trellis. With a bit of imagination, you can train climbing roses to grow in a number of different shapes to create unusual landscape effects.

One of the most visually rewarding approaches is to train the hardy rose to a vertical support (Figure 3-3). This might be a post already in the ground holding up, say, the carport, deck or veranda. Or it might be a pole that you put up specifically to support the plant. Any support can serve the purpose as long as it is very sturdy, well anchored and in full sun. To train the plant, tie the long canes tightly to the post, creating a vine effect. Tie all the canes to the support as they grow, rather than letting them become leggy and then trying to secure them. Done gradually, the job

will be less thorny and more manageable. Over the course of several weeks, the growing canes will very quickly transform the pole into a floral column or pillar, providing vibrant summer color while occupying only a few square feet of ground.

Growing in a vertical spiral, the rose will produce fewer blossoms than it would on horizontally trained canes, but its display will still be very eye-catching.

The canes produced the first year by the hardy rose can be left on the pole during the winter. During the second year, these canes will produce other canes along their length. These second-year canes can also be tied to the pole to further fill in the open spaces. (See Figure 3-1, page 48, to decide which canes

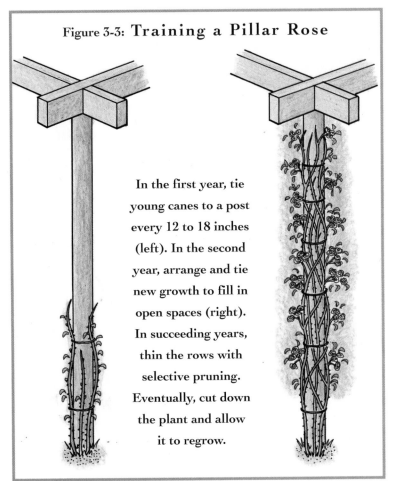

Figure 3-3: **Training a Pillar Rose**

In the first year, tie young canes to a post every 12 to 18 inches (left). In the second year, arrange and tie new growth to fill in open spaces (right). In succeeding years, thin the rows with selective pruning. Eventually, cut down the plant and allow it to regrow.

No matter how you tie a climbing rose initially, you often want to rearrange the canes.
If the ties are twine and easy to cut, the task is much simplified.

to prune out in year three and beyond.)

It will be slightly more difficult to selectively prune a pillar rose than one trained to a trellis, because of the pillar rose's compact growth. You may want to try my approach and cut the entire plant down every few years when it starts to become a tangled mess, then allow it to regrow. The alternative is to leave the framework of canes and allow the rose to branch out and occupy more space around the pole. As with many forms of ornamental horticulture, there is no right or wrong way to train a plant, only the way that seems most appropriate in your garden.

Hardy roses can also be trained into a fountain, a style of pruning that can produce a huge flowering plant easily reaching a width of 8 feet. The long, upright canes of the Explorer series roses are ideal for this kind of training, but other varieties with long, straight, sturdy canes will also grow well.

To start, allow the plant to grow as a tall shrub rose for its first summer to produce good, strong, upright canes. In the fall when the bush is dormant, look over the canes carefully and prune out all but five to seven of the strongest ones. Rake up the pruned canes and any dead foliage to eliminate a potential

With a bit of imagination, you can train a climbing rose to grow in intricate patterns.

site for disease organisms to overwinter.

Next, drive a metal fence post or sturdy stake into the ground beside the rose and tie all the remaining canes to this post. A 6-foot post driven about 2 feet into the ground works well. Tie the bush to the pole with stout twine, securing it about 18 inches up the post, at 3 feet and, again, near the top.

Allow the plant to winter in this position. In the spring, prune out any dead wood, cut the tips of the remaining canes back 6 to 8 inches and retie any canes that have come loose from the twine. The canes should be just above the top of the post.

Let the rose throw side shoots all summer, but do not allow any further main canes or suckers to develop from the ground. The bush can be shaped either into a fountain or a more blocky form, depending on whether you let shoots grow from the lower portion of

established canes, below, say, about 3 feet. If you let these shoots emerge, the bush will have a square shape. If you prune out these shoots, maintaining the original five to seven canes, and concentrate growth on the top, the bush will have a more fountainlike shape. Keep the plant well watered and fed; it will respond with a cascade of blooming canes.

Early in the third spring, prune out one-quarter or one-third of all the flowering canes that spray out from the upright growth. Cut them back at the point where they emerge from the main canes. This will force the upright growth to throw new spray canes. Keep the strongest and longest of these. Each year thereafter, remove one-quarter to one-third of the weakest growth back to the central upright canes, and enjoy the summer blooming of a floral fountain (Figure 3-4, page 55).

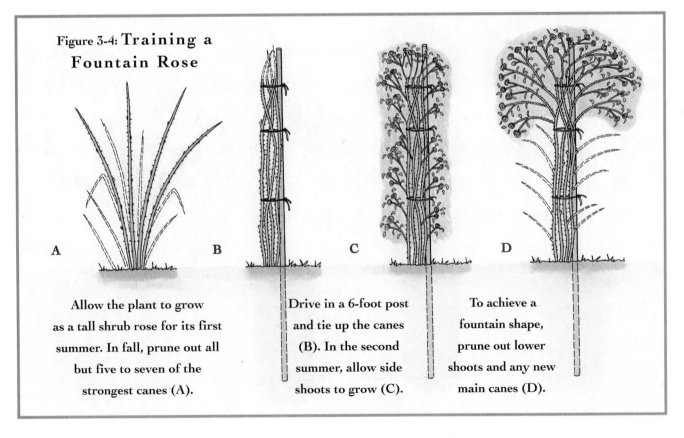

Figure 3-4: Training a Fountain Rose

A

B

C

D

Allow the plant to grow as a tall shrub rose for its first summer. In fall, prune out all but five to seven of the strongest canes (A).

Drive in a 6-foot post and tie up the canes (B). In the second summer, allow side shoots to grow (C).

To achieve a fountain shape, prune out lower shoots and any new main canes (D).

With artful pruning, a climbing rose becomes living sculpture.

In our garden, I have been experimenting with short pruning, maintaining central upright canes as low as 3 feet, and allowing the spring growth to cascade over nearby evergreen shrubs and perennials. Allowing tall perennials such as delphiniums to shoot

Five, pages 84-99, for detailed instructions on raising container-grown roses.)

One of the primary concerns with trailing roses is whether they bloom on new wood or old wood. If a plant blooms on new wood—canes that are less than a year old—it will flower the first year. If it blooms on old wood, you will have to wait for the second season before you will see a blossom.

Blooming habit is not immediately apparent from the way a rose grows. You have to be familiar with the variety or watch it for a year or two. At our farm, I learned that lesson the hard way. I planted a huge hanging basket with trailing roses and a number of other flowers. The other plants rewarded me with cascades of blossoms that first summer, but nary a rose did I see.

No matter how you grow and prune roses, bear in mind that tying up thick old canes is not a job for the faint of heart. Old canes are usually strong and uncooperative and seem to bare their thorns at the sight of soft flesh. Before starting to "tie the canes upright" as some rose books glibly phrase it, be sure to put on a long-sleeved jacket, leather gloves and a determined look. Sharp pruners and strong wrists are two other prerequisites for the job.

Artful pruning can turn a tangle of canes into living sculpture. But every bit as important as pruning is the feeding and watering you give the plant. No amount of remedial pruning will fix the thin canes or sparse blossoms due to inadequate sunlight, water or nutrition. As long as you provide the requisite care, raising roses in unconventional ways can be wonderfully rewarding.

up through the reaching canes creates a particularly dynamic summer picture. Tender climbing roses in hanging baskets can also be spectacular, as the canes, heavy with blossoms, trail over the container. (See Chapter

Rambling beauties: Rosa gallica officinalis *(above) and 'Mrs. John Laing' (right).*

Chapter Four ❧ *Shrub Roses*

Chapter Four

SHRUB ROSES

D ESPITE THEIR BIG, WOODY, RAMBLING nature, most shrub roses put forth brief flowering displays of small blossoms and clusters of blooms. Some varieties are quite sedate, adding subtle color and fragrance to the garden, while others are vibrant and commanding, like a party guest eager to be the center of attention.

Shrub roses can quickly get out of hand. They can dominate perennial borders and climb over the tops of woody ornamentals unless they are kept in check with regular pruning. With seasonal attention, they are among the most rewarding roses and are some of my favorite plants. A number of shrub roses grow outside my office windows, lending their perfume to summer mornings. I have incorporated others into our main perennial borders. There is always room for shrub roses in creative gardening.

A GENERAL DESCRIPTION OF COMMON SHRUB ROSE TYPES

NAME OF TYPE	FLOWER FORM	USE	GENERAL COMMENTS
Bourbon	Large, mostly double, repeat blooms	General use; most are very fragrant	Plant deeply; otherwise, likely to be winter damaged.
Centifolia (Cabbage)	Cluster, non-repeating	General use; most are very fragrant	Usually hardy but variable. Plant deeply.
Damascena (Damask)	Large flower but often recessed into foliage	General use; usually very fragrant	Good rose but can be tender Plant deeply.
English	Large flower, fully double, very fragrant	General, border, individual	Very popular, easily found in the trade. Plant deeply.
Gallica (French)	Cluster, non-repeating	General use; fragrance good	Usually hardy, but deep planting is a good practice.
Hybrid Foetida	Cluster, non-repeating	Bush specimens	Hardy shrub
Hybrid Musk	Cluster, small blossoms, repeat blooms	Fragrant, medium-height bush	Hardy; tolerates more shade than other roses. Plant deeply.
Hybrid Perpetuals	Large flower, repeat blooms	General, border, cutting	Plant deeply in cold areas.
Moss	Cluster, some repeat blooms	General use; usually very fragrant	Usually hardy, but plant deeply.
Moyesii	Cluster, some types repeat and some do not	Tall, bush type	Usually hardy, but should be planted deeply.
Noisette	Cluster, repeat blooms	General use; fragrant	Tender. Plant deeply.
Rugosa	Cluster	Hedges, mass plantings, light shade	Hardy. Mostly disease resistant, easy to grow.
Species	Mostly cluster, some exceptions	General use as shrubs	Hardiness varies with species. Plant deeply.

With deep planting, it is possible to grow just about any kind of rose in a cold climate. So gardeners can choose to grow shrub roses for their own merits and not because they are the only roses that will survive. Even though many shrub roses are quite hardy, they will still benefit from deep planting, especially during that one winter in ten that sends the entire garden to the deep freeze. (For a description of how to deep-plant roses from different types of containers, see Chapter Two, pages 31-37.)

The tables in this chapter will help gardeners pick shrub roses appropriate for their settings. The most common types are listed with their flowering habits and suggestions for planting. Unfortunately, with the exception of the English roses, shrub types are not readily available at garden centers and must be purchased through mail-order nurseries. The roses described here are included in part because they are all available through the mail-order trade (see Resources, page 117, for a short list of sources).

Gardeners with access to the Internet might want to visit the newsgroup rec.gardens.rose or rec.gardens, as there is often a lively debate about the merits of different mail-order suppliers. Reading about shrub roses is certainly useful in making informed decisions about what types would suit your landscape. Visiting an arboretum or formal rose garden to see various types in bloom and after flowering is even more instructive.

Even though shrub roses are quite hardy, they will still benefit from deep planting.

BOURBON
Rosa x *borboniana*

BOURBON ROSES ARE THOUGHT TO be a cross between the hybrid China roses and a branch of the damask family. While there are other ancestors in the breeding line, these are believed to be the primary parent stock. The hybrid China parentage results in repeat blooming but creates winter tenderness. These are interesting roses with excellent fragrance. They should be planted deeply to ensure long-term survival.

CENTIFOLIA
Rosa x *centifolia*

THE GROWTH OF THE CENTIFOLIA ROSE is more open and sprawling than many of the other shrub rose classes. With its sprawling habit and thorny stems, the centifolia often benefits from staking or close planting to hold it more upright.

In a shrub border, these roses do very well planted close to other plants that support them. Hardy in most winters in our Zone 4 garden, they will suffer cane burn in a severe winter. Deep planting is not usually necessary but is recommended. Varieties such as 'Fantin-Latour' have been winter damaged more than should be expected from catalog descriptions; it is probable that there is some tender China rose in its genealogy. The flower stalks of centifolia roses often have difficulty holding the weight of the flower heads. Gardeners will soon get used to turning over the delightfully scented blossoms to view the colors.

DAMASCENA
Rosa x *damascena*

THE DAMASK ROSES HAVE A complex genealogy and seem to be a mixture of *Rosa moschata*, *R. gallica* and *R. phoenicia* (and possibly other spontaneous seedlings in the mix). They do not have a well-defined family characteristic for height, fragrance or flower form. The most pronounced of the characteristics would include a gray tone to the foliage and medium-thorny wood stalks. Many of the damask roses have weak stalks that allow the heavily laden blossoms to droop. We deep-plant the damask roses in our collection.

ENGLISH ROSE

THE ENGLISH ROSE, A CROSS BETWEEN the modern hybrid roses and selected older shrub roses, has produced some very attractive and fragrant plants. The originator of this class, David Austin, has been introducing these roses since the early 1960s. Con-

'Graham Thomas' is a fragrant English rose that reaches a height of about 4 feet.

Named for English horticulturist Gertrude Jekyll, this fragrant rose honors her achievements.

BOURBON AND CENTIFOLIA ROSES

NAME	FLOWER FORM	HEIGHT	BOUQUET	COLOR
BOURBON				
Boule de Neige	Fully double	5 feet	Extremely fragrant	White
Bourbon Queen	Double	6 feet	Extremely fragrant	Mid-pink
Commandant Beaurepaire	Double	5 feet	Extremely fragrant	Rose-pink with purplish stripe
Honorine de Brabant	Double	5 feet	Extremely fragrant	Pink with purplish stripe
Kathleen Harrop	Double	6 feet	Extremely fragrant	Light pink
Louise Odier	Fully double	6 feet	Extremely fragrant	Deep pink
Mme. Ernst Calvat	Double	6 feet	Extremely fragrant	Mid-pink
Mme. Isaac Pereire	Fully double	6 feet	Extremely fragrant	Deep pink
Mme. Lauriol de Barny	Fully double	5 feet	Extremely fragrant	Light pink
Mme. Pierre Oger	Double	4 feet	Extremely fragrant	Pink shades
Souvenir de la Malmaison	Fully double	2 feet	Extremely fragrant	Light pink
Souvenir de St. Anne's	Semi-double	3 feet	Extremely fragrant	Light pink
Variegata di Bologna	Fully double	5 feet	Extremely fragrant	White with purplish stripe
Zéphirine Drouhin	Semi-double	6 feet	Extremely fragrant	Mid-pink
CENTIFOLIA				
Blanchefleur	Fully double	4 feet	Extremely fragrant	Blush pink
Bullata	Fully double	4 feet	Extremely fragrant	Deep pink
De Meaux	Double	4 feet	Extremely fragrant	Mid-pink
Duc de Fitzjames	Fully double	4 feet	Extremely fragrant	Deep red
Fantin-Latour	Fully double	4 feet	Extremely fragrant	Light pink
Juno	Fully double	4 feet	Extremely fragrant	Light pink
La Noblesse	Double	4 feet	Extremely fragrant	Light pink
Paul Ricault	Fully double	5 feet	Extremely fragrant	Deep pink
Petite de Hollande	Fully double	4 feet	Extremely fragrant	Mid-pink
Robert le Diable	Fully double	3 feet	Extremely fragrant	Scarlet to purple
Rose des Peintres	Fully double	5 feet	Extremely fragrant	Mid-pink
The Bishop	Fully double	4 feet	Extremely fragrant	Mauve
Tour de Malakoff	Fully double	5 feet	Extremely fragrant	Mauve-pink

DAMASCENA AND ENGLISH ROSES

NAME	FLOWER FORM	HEIGHT	BOUQUET	COLOR
DAMASCENA				
Arthur de Sansal	Fully double	2 feet	Extremely fragrant	Deep red
Blanc de Vibert	Fully double	7 feet	Extremely fragrant	White
Celsiana	Double	4 feet	Extremely fragrant	Light pink
Four Seasons	Double	4 feet	Extremely fragrant	Deep pink
Hebe's Lip	Semi-double	5 feet	Extremely fragrant	Light pink
Ispahan	Fully double	5 feet	Extremely fragrant	Mid-pink
Jacques Cartier	Fully double	4 feet	Extremely fragrant	Mid-pink
Leda	Fully double	5 feet	Extremely fragrant	Light pink
Mme. Hardy	Fully double	5 feet	Extremely fragrant	White
Mme. Zöetmans	Fully double	4 feet	Extremely fragrant	White
Omar Khayyam	Double	4 feet	Extremely fragrant	Light pink
Panachée de Lyon	Double	4 feet	Extremely fragrant	Pink shades
Pergolèse	Fully double	3 feet	Extremely fragrant	Wine-red
St. Nicholas	Semi-double	3 feet	Extremely fragrant	Deep pink
ENGLISH ROSES				
Charles Austin	Double	5 feet	Extremely fragrant	Apricot blend
Ellen	Fully double	4 feet	Extremely fragrant	Apricot blend
Evelyn	Fully double	3½ feet	Extremely fragrant	Apricot blend
Fair Bianca	Fully double	3 feet	Very fragrant	White
Gertrude Jekyll	Fully double	4 feet	Extremely fragrant	Mid-pink
Graham Thomas	Double	4 feet	Extremely fragrant	Deep yellow
Heritage	Double	4 feet	Extremely fragrant	Light pink
Leander	Fully double	6 feet	Extremely fragrant	Apricot blend
Mary Rose	Fully double	4 feet	Extremely fragrant	Mid-pink
Mary Webb	Double	4 feet	Very fragrant	Light yellow
Pretty Jessica	Fully double	2½ feet	Extremely fragrant	Mid-pink
Sharifa Asma	Fully double	3 feet	Extremely fragrant	Light pink
Swan	Fully double	4 feet	Very fragrant	White
The Yeoman	Fully double	3 feet	Extremely fragrant	Mid-pink
William Shakespeare	Fully double	3½ feet	Extremely fragrant	Deep red
Yellow Charles Austin	Double	5 feet	Very fragrant	Mid-yellow

GALLICA ROSES

NAME	FLOWER FORM	HEIGHT	BOUQUET	COLOR
Alain Blanchard	Semi-double	4 feet	Extremely fragrant	Red shades
Anaïs Segalas	Double	3 feet	Extremely fragrant	Mid-pink
Apothecary's Rose sp. *R. gallica*	Semi-double	3 feet	Extremely fragrant	Deep pink
Assemblage des Beautés	Fully double	4 feet	Extremely fragrant	Deep red
Belle de Crécy	Fully double	4 feet	Extremely fragrant	Purple-red
Belle Isis	Double	4 feet	Extremely fragrant	Light pink
Brennus	Fully double	4 feet	Good fragrance	Deep red
Cardinal de Richelieu	Fully double	4 feet	Extremely fragrant	Maroon-purple
Charles de Mills	Fully double	4 feet	Extremely fragrant	Mauve
Cosimo Ridolfi	Fully double	4 feet	Good fragrance	Violet
Duchesse de Buccleugh	Double	4 feet	Extremely fragrant	Red shades
Du Maître d'Ecole	Fully double	3 feet	Extremely fragrant	Mauve
Empress Josephine	Fully double	4 feet	Extremely fragrant	Mid-pink
Ipsilanté	Fully Double	4 feet	Extremely fragrant	Lilac-pink
Nestor	Double	4 feet	Extremely fragrant	Mid-red
Surpasse Tout	Double	3 feet	Extremely fragrant	Mid-red
Tuscany Superb	Fully double	4 feet	Extremely fragrant	Crimson-purple

sequently, they are sometimes referred to as Austin roses. The flowers are, for the most part, fully double and extremely fragrant and are worth a place in any garden. Grow these repeat-blooming roses by themselves or plant them in a general border where they will happily coexist with perennials. One of our garden's most popular combinations is a yellow 'Graham Thomas' interplanted with violet delphiniums. Although not for the faint of heart, this color combination is pleasing to many visitors.

I have found that although they are hardier than originally thought, the canes of English roses usually suffer winter damage in our Zone 4 garden. I follow the deep planting method with these roses, and I have yet to lose one. I don't prune these plants back quite so hard as hybrid tea roses in the hope that the canes will survive the cold and resume vigorous growth early in the spring.

The table on page 65 highlights the most popular and available varieties. This is not meant to be an all-inclusive list of English roses, but it provides the reader with the important characteristics of individual types.

*Gallicas like 'Tuscany Superb' are hardy,
self-tending roses that tolerate some shade.*

GALLICA
Rosa gallica

THE GALLICA ROSES ARE FOR THE most part quite hardy and do not require deep planting for ensured survival. These are roses for those who wish to follow the dictum of "plant and ignore." Easily grown, this class lives on any type of soil, although the better the soil, the more abundant the flowers. Gallicas are also one of the few roses that will tolerate shade. Tolerance does not imply great performance, but some shade is not as damaging to this class as to

other classes of rose. The flower stalks hold the fragrant blossoms upright. The colors tend toward pink, mauve and red. Striped blooms are also common. The gallicas sucker freely in good soil and will have to be controlled.

HYBRID FOETIDA
Rosa foetida
'Harison's Yellow'

THIS SINGLE ROSE IS MENtioned because it is found throughout our northeast region in the oldest gardens or around old stone foundations. Bred in 1830 in the United States, 'Harison's Yellow' is a thorny, non-repeating bloomer that suckers crazily around the garden, forming an impenetrable mass of canes. The fragrance is sweetly agreeable on the bright yellow blossoms and it makes a glorious but all-too-brief summer show. This is an excellent rose for the historic garden with a large planting area.

HYBRID MUSK
Rosa moschata

THIS COLLECTION OF ROSES SHARES several characteristics: All are fragrant, with a rather sweet, fruity perfume. My own scent preference leans heavily to the perfume generated by musk roses. With a few exceptions, they are not for the small garden, as the plants can be quite large and aggressive. The shorter plants in the table on page 69 would

With its sweet fragrance, 'Harison's Yellow' makes a glorious but brief summer show.

Chapter Four ❧ *Shrub Roses*

HYBRID MUSK ROSES

NAME	FLOWER FORM	HEIGHT	BOUQUET	COLOR
Ballerina	Single	3 feet	Good fragrance	Mid-pink
Bishop Darlington	Semi-double	4 feet	Extremely fragrant	Pink shades
Buff Beauty	Double	5 feet	Extremely fragrant	Yellow shades
Clytemnestra	Single	6 feet	Extremely fragrant	Orange-pink
Cornelia	Semi-double	5 feet	Good fragrance	Pink shades
Danaë	Double	5 feet	Good fragrance	Light yellow
Daybreak	Semi-double	4 feet	Extremely fragrant	Mid-yellow
Felicia	Semi-double	4 feet	Extremely fragrant	Pink shades
Francesca	Semi-double	5 feet	Extremely fragrant	Apricot blends
Kathleen	Single	4 feet	Good fragrance	Light pink
Moonlight	Semi-double	5 feet	Good fragrance	White
Nur Mahal	Semi-double	4 feet	Extremely fragrant	Mid-red
Pax	Semi-double	5 feet	Extremely fragrant	White
Penelope	Double	6 feet	Extremely fragrant	Light pink
Prosperity	Double	6 feet	Extremely fragrant	White
Queen of the Musks	Double	3 feet	Extremely fragrant	Pink shades
Thisbe	Semi-double	4 feet	Extremely fragrant	Mid-yellow
Vanity	Single	6 feet	Good fragrance	Deep pink

be more acceptable in a small garden. Although hybrid musks are quite hardy, we follow the deep planting method and set the graft, or bud union, 6 inches below ground. This does lead to suckering, but since the suckers are genetically similar to the tops, they do not have to be removed. In fact, because the foliage of some varieties is sparse, the suckers add to the fullness and overall appearance of the plant.

Despite its fragrance and everblooming habit, this class of shrub rose has never become very popular, which I find quite surprising.

HYBRID PERPETUALS

THE HYBRID PERPETUAL ROSES CAME into existence in the mid-1800s when tender China roses with their repeat-blooming characteristic were bred with roses such as the damasks and bourbons. The resulting hybrids combined the repeat blooming of the China rose with the double flower and fragrance of their mates. The resulting rose was more tender than its parent stock, but the public bought all they could find because of the new hybrid's repeat-blooming habit. The hybrid perpetuals in turn gave way to the

Repeat-blooming hybrid perpetuals, such as 'John Hopper', captured the hearts of gardeners when the roses were introduced in the mid-1800s.

superior blooming qualities of the hybrid teas when they were widely introduced to the gardening world.

The hybrid perpetual is a vigorous rose; the canes can often reach a length of 6 feet in a single year. Hardiness is variable in this class because of the inherited characteristics of the tender China rose, but deep planting ensures survival in the toughest winter. If the canes do die back in a hard winter, merely prune them close to the ground in the spring. The new canes will grow and flower in the same year, without losing a blooming season. To increase flowering, stretch canes as horizontally as possible by tying them to a fence, shrub or evergreen. Horizontal canes will produce blooms along their length, while canes left upright will tend to produce blooms only at the tip.

In their heyday, hybrid perpetuals were extremely popular and were available in thousands of varieties. Now, relatively few varieties remain. The accompanying table lists only a fraction of those, but they are varieties easily found in the mail-order trade. Note that the height of the plants is a rough approximation and will vary depending on climate and soils.

HYBRID PERPETUAL ROSES

NAME	FLOWER FORM	HEIGHT	BOUQUET	COLOR
Alfred Colomb	Double	5 feet	Extremely fragrant	Deep red
Baron Girod de l'Ain	Double	5 feet	Extremely fragrant	Crimson with white edge
Baronne Prévost	Double	4 feet	Extremely fragrant	Mid-pink
Empereur du Maroc	Double	4 feet	Extremely fragrant	Deep red
Eugène Fürst	Double	5 feet	Extremely fragrant	Deep red
Ferdinand Pichard	Double	4 feet	Extremely fragrant	Pink, striped crimson
Fisher Holmes	Double	5 feet	Good fragrance	Purplish red
Frau Karl Druschki	Double	6 feet	Good fragrance	white
Général Jacqueminot	Double	5 feet	Good fragrance	Red blend
General Washington	Double	6 feet	Good fragrance	Mid-red
Georg Arends	Double	6 feet	Extremely fragrant	Mid-pink
Gloire de Ducher	Double	5 feet	Extremely fragrant	Deep red
Henry Nevard	Double	6 feet	Extremely fragrant	Deep red
Hugh Dickson	Double	6 feet	Good fragrance	Mid-red
John Hopper	Double	6 feet	Extremely fragrant	Pink range
Mabel Morrison	Double	5 feet	Good fragrance	White
Mrs. John Laing	Double	6 feet	Extremely fragrant	Mid-pink
Paul Neyron	Double	6 feet	Extremely fragrant	Mid-pink
Reine des Violettes	Double	6 feet	Extremely fragrant	Violet-red to purple
Roger Lambelin	Double	6 feet	Good fragrance	Red and white fringed petals
Souvenir du Dr. Jamain	Double	5 feet	Extremely fragrant	Deep red
Ulrich Brunner	Double	6 feet	Extremely fragrant	Deep red

MOSS ROSES

THE MOSS ROSES ARE A BRANCH OF the centifolia that are easily identifiable by the pattern of their flowers. The sepals are always arranged so that some of them lie over and some lie under neighboring sepals. While an attractive rose, it never became popular, because it was introduced at the same time as the repeat-blooming China rose. This lack of popularity may be justified. Many other roses offer more fragrance and more conspicuous blooming. On its behalf, however, I must say that the unique petal arrangement of its flowers produces a table bouquet that few other roses can match.

The unique petal arrangement of moss roses like this 'Henri Martin' create a striking bouquet.

MOSS AND MOYESII ROSES

NAME	FLOWER FORM	HEIGHT	BOUQUET	COLOR
MOSS ROSES				
Alfred de Dalmas	Semi-double	3 feet	Extremely fragrant	White
Blanche Moreau	Double	5 feet	Extremely fragrant	White
Capitaine John Ingram	Fully double	5 feet	Extremely fragrant	Deep red
Comtesse de Murinais	Double	5 feet	Extremely fragrant	White
Crested Moss	Fully double	5 feet	Extremely fragrant	Mid-pink
Deuil de Paul Fontaine	Double	4 feet	Extremely fragrant	Purplish red
Duchesse de Verneuil	Double	4 feet	Extremely fragrant	Pink shades
Eugenie Guinoisseau	Double	5 feet	Extremely fragrant	Mid-red
Général Kléber	Fully double	5 feet	Extremely fragrant	Mid-pink
Gloire des Mousseux	Fully double	4 feet	Extremely fragrant	Mid-pink
Henri Martin	Semi-double	5 feet	Extremely fragrant	Mid-red
Louis Gimard	Fully double	5 feet	Extremely fragrant	Mid-pink
Maréchal Davoust	Fully double	4 feet	Extremely fragrant	Deep pink
Marie de Blois	Double	4 feet	Good fragrance	Mid-pink
Mme. de la Roche-Lambert	Fully double	4 feet	Extremely fragrant	Deep red
Mme. Louis Lévêque	Fully double	4 feet	Extremely fragrant	Mid-pink
Nuits de Young	Double	4 feet	Extremely fragrant	Maroon-purple
William Lobb	Double	6 feet	Extremely fragrant	Purplish red
MOYESII				
Fargesii	Single	7 feet	None	Mid-red
Geranium	Single	8 feet	Slight	Mid-red
Margeurite Hilling	Single	6 feet	Medium	Mid-pink
Superba sp.	Single	8 feet	Medium	Mid-red

MOYESII
Rosa moyesii

BECAUSE THEY ARE SUCH TALL, GANGLY rambling plants and because they are not particularly fragrant, Moyesii roses are not commonly grown in modern gardens.

This class of roses was introduced from Western China by the English plant explorer E.H. "Chinese" Wilson in 1908. What sustains its appeal to certain gardeners is its remarkable blood-red color and hardiness. Also, the plants abundantly bear large, good-quality rose hips, a valuable source of vitamin C.

Moyesii roses are distinguished by their blood-red color and large, attractive rose hips.

NOISETTE
Rosa x *noisettiana*

In TENDER CLIMATES, THE NOISETTE roses can be used as tall, fragrant climbers, but in colder areas, their habit of growing late into the fall without hardening off inevitably means that the canes will die back. The honor of breeding the initial rose in this class is given to John Champneys, a rice planter in Charleston, South Carolina. He crossed a 'Miller's White Musk' with pollen from the brand-new (at the time) 'Parson's Pink China' that he received from the Noisette rose breeders in France, and in about 1802, he arrived at a hybrid he called *Rosa moschata hybrida.* It became known to the gardening public as 'Champneys' Pink Cluster'. A few years later, the French nurseryman Philippe Noisette obtained some seeds of this hybrid and planted them. The seedlings became the Noisette class of roses and were distributed throughout Europe by the Noisette family nursery in the early 1820s.

These roses tend to have tall gangly canes with good to excellent musk rose fragrance. All bloom throughout the season. If they were not so tender, they would have stolen our northern hearts.

The heights given on page 76 indicate how high the canes would grow if they survived from year to year. It is largely irrelevant for northern gardeners, because the canes will likely die to the ground every year in cold gardens. Subsequent spring cane growth will be tall, at least 5 feet of growth per year in good soils. This rose requires deep planting for winter survival.

RUGOSA ROSES
Rosa rugosa

RUGOSA ROSES NEED A PUBLIC relations director. They are underappreciated. Many gardeners have heard that *R. rugosa* is used as a rootstock for roses or that the blossoms lack the formal grace and flower show quality of hybrid teas. To correct such misinformation, it should be noted that

Rugosa roses thrive on ocean mist and sandy soil to beautify many coastal settings.

NOISETTE AND RUGOSA ROSES

NAME	FLOWER FORM	HEIGHT	BOUQUET	COLOR
NOISETTE				
Aimée Vibert	Double	12 feet	Extremely fragrant	White
Blanc Pur	Semi-double	10 feet	Good fragrance	White
Blush Noisette	Double	5 feet	Extremely fragrant	Light pink
Bouquet d'Or	Double	10 feet	Extremely fragrant	Light buff yellow
Fellenberg	Double	5 feet	Good fragrance	Mid-red
Jaune Desprez	Double	20 feet	Extremely fragrant	Yellow blends
Meteor	Double	7 feet	Extremely fragrant	Mid-red
Rêve d'Or	Semi-double	10 feet	Extremely fragrant	Mid-yellow
RUGOSA				
Alba	Single	6 feet	Very fragrant	White
Conrad F. Meyer	Double	8 feet; train as climber	Extremely fragrant	Mid-pink
David Thompson (Explorer series)	Double	4 feet	Very fragrant	Mid-red
F.J. Grootendorst	Semi-double, fringed petals	6 feet	Very little fragrance	Mid-red
Hansa	Double	6 feet	Extremely fragrant	Violet-red
Henry Hudson (Explorer series)	Double	3 feet	Extremely fragrant	White
Jens Munk (Explorer series)	Double	6 feet	Extremely fragrant	Mid-pink
Martin Frobisher (Explorer series)	Semi-double	6 feet	Very fragrant	Light-pink
Max Graf	Single	2 feet	Very fragrant	Pale pink
Nova Zembla	Double	8 feet	Extremely fragrant	Light pink
Rubra	Single	6 feet	Very fragrant	Violet-red

the rugosa used as rootstock was bred especially for that purpose and could hardly be expected to produce flowers. Other varieties yield beautiful blossoms, even though they are not the double blossoms borne on long stalks favored by judges at flower shows.

Additionally, the flowering varieties are extremely hardy, unkillable in all but the most northerly gardens. They can be planted in a row to serve as a dense, impenetrable hedge. They are disease-free and rarely bothered by insects. This rose produces an abundance of

SPECIES ROSES

NAME	FLOWER FORM	HEIGHT	BOUQUET	COLOR
Rosa blanda (Labrador Rose)	Single	5 feet	Slight fragrance	Mid-pink
R. carolina (Pasture Rose)	Single	5 feet	Extremely fragrant	Light pink
R. eglanteria (Sweet Briar Rose)	Single	8 feet	Good fragrance	Light pink
R. foetida bicolor (Austrian Copper Rose)	Single	6 feet	Good fragrance	Orange blends
R. glauca	Single	8 feet	Slight to no fragrance	Pink blend
R. moschata (Musk Rose)	Single	8 feet	Extremely fragrant	White
R. woodsii fendlerii (Western Rose)	Single	4 feet	Good fragrance	Mid-pink

flowers in almost any soil, from heavy clay to beach sand. Rugosas bloom for a long period and bear either single or double blossoms with wonderful fragrance. After the petals fall, the plants produce rose hips, or seedpods, of a deep red-orange. Attractive in themselves, they are also useful in cosmetics and in food as a rich source of vitamin C.

Rugosas do have a few less-attractive characteristics. They are a prickly rose, heavily armored with unforgiving thorns. And they sucker and can spread throughout the garden, a tendency that may need to be curtailed by digging out the suckers in midsummer. The rugosa's wandering characteristic can be an asset if you are trying to stabilize steep bankings or open areas. I have planted quite a few rugosas around our large irrigation pond to hold the banks against erosion.

The table on page 76 lists some of the rugosa roses currently available.

SPECIES ROSES

SPECIES ROSES ARE NOT THE RESULT of extensive breeding. They have been adopted from nature. They are nonhybrids, close to their natural state. Species roses are for the adventurous, for collectors or for those with very large gardens and room to spare. While I acknowledge the current popularity of collecting these roses and the enthusiasm of their supporters, my experience is that there are better garden performers than the species. A few have grown well in our garden, but they have drawn less-than-enthusiastic reviews for flower or fragrance. One of the main drawbacks with the true species roses is their relatively short bloom time. A *Rosa glauca* (synonym *Rosa rubrifolia*) only blooms in our garden for a little more than a week. While its two-toned pink single blossoms are stunning, the plant lives the rest of the sum-

The fragrant single blooms of 'Austrian Copper' are borne on canes that can reach 6 feet.

Chapter Four ❧ *Shrub Roses*

Figure 4-1: How Shrub Roses Grow

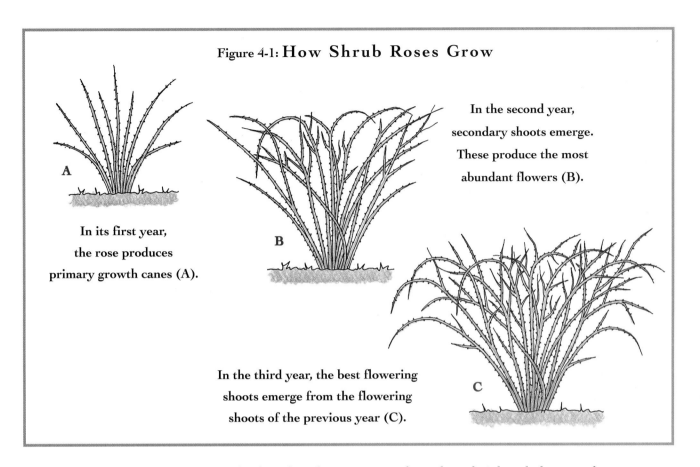

A

In its first year,
the rose produces
primary growth canes (A).

B

In the second year,
secondary shoots emerge.
These produce the most
abundant flowers (B).

C

In the third year, the best flowering
shoots emerge from the flowering
shoots of the previous year (C).

mer as a tall coppery green shrub. When the rose hips develop and take on a deep red-orange, the plant again becomes ornamental. Species roses can be an asset to your landscape as long as their size, shape and seasonal appearance fit your overall design. If your interest lies in long-season blooms or haunting fragrances, particularly in small gardens, there are better roses. The table on page *77* lists some of the more attractive and readily available types.

MAINTENANCE PRUNING

PRUNING SHRUB ROSES IS EASIER ONCE you understand how they grow (Figure 4-1). These roses tend to throw thick canes that flower in their first year. These large canes overwinter, then produce secondary canes from along their length the second year. It is these secondary canes that are the heaviest blooming and most desirable. If these secondary canes are allowed to remain on the rose for the winter, they in turn will produce canes from along their length. These third-year canes will also produce flowers, but the canes will be thinner than the second-year canes and will not support the weight of a heavy crop of flowers. This process will continue, with each year's canes producing a new crop of flowering canes, until the plant becomes an unruly mass of dead and dying canes mixed with overgrown and often spindly flower-producing canes.

To keep this plant vigorous and flowering, every spring prune out one-third of all large canes at the base of the rose. Prune out the oldest canes, those that are starting to produce either the three- or four-year canes. If this is done every year, the rose will have an equal number (or close to it) of first-, second- and third-year canes producing flowers. This pattern of pruning will ensure a continual supply of high-quality blooms (Figure 4-2).

If the rose is producing suckers, dig them out as they appear throughout the summer. If the suckers are allowed to grow, the plant will become a monster requiring drastic renovation.

Summer pruning of shrub roses is quite simple. Take off the dying blossoms. This removes the source of food for botrytis fungus and tidies up the plant. It is a good habit to wander through the garden every day and hand-pluck the dying blossoms. Take a firm grip on each blossom and strip off all the dying petals. The seedpods can be left on to form rose hips, giving the garden some orange or red-orange fall color. Or, once all the petals are gone, you can simply prune off the remains of the flower clusters along with the seedpods.

Summer pruning resembles housecleaning. You do it for orderliness, health and peace of mind.

RENOVATION

PRUNING LARGE SHRUB ROSES IS A JOB that is too easy to put off. These plants fight back with numerous sharp thorns. We put off the task until one day we note that the plant is not blooming as heavily as we remember or it has grown into a monster and is threatening to take over the entire garden. Instead of a yearly maintenance task, we are now faced with a renovation job (Figure 4-3).

There are several ways to proceed. If the

Figure 4-2: Maintenance Pruning

To keep a shrub rose flowering prolifically, prune out one-third of all large canes at the base of the rose every spring.

rose is on its own roots, has developed a massive central core of thick old canes and is throwing suckers, cut the entire mess to the ground. Most roses, except hybrid teas and floribundas, will become established on their own roots if deeply planted. To cut back an overgrown plant, you can rent a metal-bladed weed trimmer and quickly reduce the rosebush to a dense, woody stump 3 to 6 inches high. Remember, though, that uncontrolled, this tool can take a very large bite out of legs, ankles or toes. Work safely and follow directions.

Once most of the bush has been chopped down, it is easy to dig out the remnants of the small canes that have escaped the trimmer and consign them to the dump or shredder. The following spring, when new canes emerge from the roots, pick three to seven of the strongest ones as the core of the bush. Dig out all the others. I suggest digging, because pruning at ground level only encourages more shoots to develop from the roots.

If renovation pruning is undertaken in the early spring before the buds start to swell, the rose will be back at full strength and blooming later in the season. The job can also be undertaken in the late fall.

Whether in spring or fall, make sure the rose is dormant before cutting. Dormancy in the fall is evidenced by the loss of leaves. Once the foliage turns color and starts to drop off, the plant is entering dormancy. In the spring, the plant is out of dormancy when the buds start to swell.

Pruning too early in the fall will stimulate new growth that will not harden enough to survive the winter. Pruning too late in the spring removes the energy and buds already produced by the plant, which will weaken the rosebush and reduce its flowering.

If the plant has not become established on its own roots—due to growing conditions or its young age—and has become a mass of overgrown canes emerging from one central point, take heavy pruning shears in hand and try this approach:

First, remove all dead wood. Dead canes can be identified by the dark color of the bark. The bark may also be split and peeling. If you are in doubt as to the vitality of a cane, make a small scratch and peel the bark away. If the layer under the bark is brown, the cane is dead. If this layer is green, the cane is alive. If the cane is alive but is old and dark, it might be better to remove it and make way for newer, more vigorous growth.

Then remove all large crossing or rubbing branches, especially from the interior of the rosebush. To do this, choose which of the two branches is to be removed, generally the older of the pair, and cut it back to the point where it originated as a bud. If it starts from the ground, cut it to the ground. If it starts half-

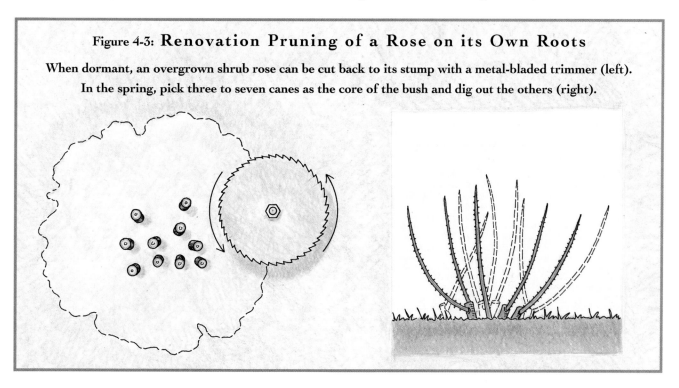

Figure 4-3: Renovation Pruning of a Rose on its Own Roots
When dormant, an overgrown shrub rose can be cut back to its stump with a metal-bladed trimmer (left). In the spring, pick three to seven canes as the core of the bush and dig out the others (right).

Shrub roses like 'Rosa Mundi' are forgiving plants. Any mispruning will be covered by new growth.

way up a cane, cut it back to this spot.

For beginners, the encouraging news about renovation pruning is that the shrub rose is a forgiving plant. Even if the gardener makes a mistake, the rose will quickly regrow another cane (or twenty).

Prune out all overcrowded areas to thin the rose and improve air circulation. Thinning allows the remaining canes to become stronger and better able to support all those new blooms that will be produced as a result of this pruning.

Prune out all weak or spindly branches. If a branch is unable to support the weight of a cluster of blossoms without bending, remove it.

Finally, cut all the remaining canes to half their height. Sometimes these long arching canes do not produce many blossoms, and shortening their height forces them to throw new flower-producing side shoots. If this seems like too much pruning in one season, cut back only half the canes in the first year. Watch the resulting new growth. If it creates more flowers and a more attractive plant, finish the job the following spring.

Having renovated many shrub roses, I know that it is much easier to maintain these woody shrubs than to bring them back from an overgrown state. I suspect this is a lesson you will learn yourself.

Hybrid musks, including 'Belinda', can be large and aggressive and need room to ramble.

Chapter Five

ROSES *in* CONTAINERS

A NY KIND OF ROSE CAN BE CONSIDERED FOR container growing, so let your imagination roam. In our large gardens, I grow a climbing variety called 'Blaze' in a hanging basket and raise many hybrid teas in clay pots of several different sizes. Friends grow entire gardens of miniature roses on their apartment balconies. Although by reputation roses are challenging to raise, in reality they are quite adaptable and can be grown wherever you would like their fragrance and beauty.

The conditions for success are narrower in container culture than when raising roses in the ground, and fatal mistakes are easier to make. Attentive watering is certainly critical, as is a good soil mix and the proper container. But with some planning and effort, you can succeed with almost any rose and enjoy a bit of paradise in a pot.

I grow 'Blaze' (left) in a hanging basket and enjoy the look of a hybrid tea (above) among annuals.

*Wooden pots work well for container gardening because they absorb moisture and provide
a layer of damp material between the root ball and the surrounding air.*

CONTAINERS

ONE OF THE FIRST CONSIDERATIONS for patio roses is choosing a suitable container. It must be large enough for the ultimate size of the plant and have an opening in the bottom for drainage. And it needs to be large enough to accommodate healthy root development, or the plant will become pot-bound and stunted. Although space is usually a consideration in most container gardens, as far as the plants are concerned, there is no such thing as too large a container. We have found that containers with a capacity of 5 to

6 gallons support excellent rose growth and blooming through an average summer.

Pots of 5 gallons or larger help moderate fluctuations in soil temperature. Gardeners tend to forget that summer heat, while wonderful for foliage and flowers, can be deadly to the roots of container-grown plants. Deep in the ground, roots are protected from wild daily swings in temperature. The ground slowly heats up over the summer and the roots gradually adjust. The larger the container, the more gradual the temperature change.

Likewise, the color of the container can be

important in moderating heat and ensuring root survival, especially in plastic pots. Light tones absorb less heat than dark colors and so create a more root-friendly environment.

Smaller containers, with a capacity of less than, say, 3 gallons, offer very little insulation to the roots and hold relatively little moisture. They may have to be watered once or twice a day, depending on the size and water needs of the plants. Smaller pots are also lighter, especially if your soil mix contains a lot of peat, and they are apt to tip over in the slightest breeze.

In my experience, the best containers are made of clay or wood. Unlike, say, plastic, clay and wood do not heat up very quickly in direct sunlight. They insulate the soil and protect the plant's small feeder roots. Because clay and wood absorb water, they also provide a layer of damp material between the root ball and the surrounding air. When the sun heats the pot, moisture in the walls of the container evaporates and cools the soil. The large clay pots often prominent in pictures of famous gardens are testimony to their superior qualities. The best gardeners choose the best containers. Clay pots are ideal for plants, and they are attractive and enhance the appearance of any setting.

I have also grown roses in the small fiber pots used by many retailers. They are inexpensive and can support rose growth, but they are not ideal, as they must be watered once or twice a day.

Containers can be in the form of baskets as well as pots. Hanging baskets can support some spectacular roses. One of our most eye-catching arrangements includes a basket-

grown 'Blaze' climbing rose at its center. The rose canes arch out at least 6 feet and give blooms for most of the summer. The basket is quite large, 12 to 15 gallons or about 3 feet in diameter, and is planted with a different cast of annual flowers each summer to set off the deep red blossoms of the rose.

Smaller baskets can be used as well, but anything less than 3 gallons or a diameter of 16 inches or so is probably too small to hold sufficient moisture.

My large basket is made of bent wire and has a coco lining to hold the soil. Such sizable

Ceramic pots are ideal for plants and enhance the appearance of any setting.

Figure 5-1: **Hanging Baskets**

Large wire baskets can hold a rose as well as annual flowers. Line the wire frame with coco matting or sphagnum moss. Cover the lining with plastic and poke a drainage hole in the center before adding the growing medium.

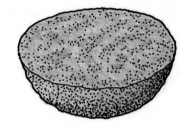

Growing Medium

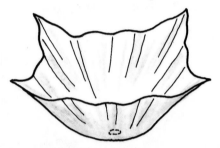

Plastic with Drain Hole

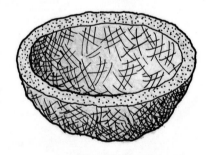

Fiber Lining

Bent-Wire Basket

containers may be difficult to find, but they are worth the search because they can be used to create some remarkable plantings. Specialty garden centers can usually obtain the baskets and the coco lining. Some gardeners use long fiber sphagnum moss as a liner; however, moss is more time consuming to work with than coco matting.

Whatever the matting, after you have it in place on the bottom of the basket, put a piece of plastic, cut to fit, on top of it. You can use a piece of a garbage bag, black plastic or clear plastic. It doesn't matter—it won't show, since it will be covered with your soil mix. The plastic will extend the life of the matting for three to five years, reduce evaporation and help the rose grow unchecked by water stress or excessive heat in the root zone. To keep the soil from becoming soggy, remember to poke a finger-sized drainage hole in the plastic (Figure 5-1).

PLANTING MIXES

GOOD CONTAINER SOIL IS DIFFERENT from garden soil. Thinking about containers for a moment will illustrate why this is so. Gardeners water their containers with a hose or watering can and often apply an inch or two of water, enough to fill up the pot, in 30 seconds or less. Imagine the force of a rainstorm that dumped an inch or two of water on the garden in the same 30 seconds. It would compact the ground like a steam roller. It can have the same effect on a container if the potting mix is not loose and resistant to compaction.

Compacted soil has little or no air, which plant roots need, while good soil is composed of 20 to 25 percent air by volume. Sufficient air space also promotes good drainage and fertilizer uptake. If the air spaces are squeezed out by soil compaction when the container is watered, a plant's roots will eventually suffocate. A loose soil mix is essential for good container roses.

A lightweight mix is also important. Containers are like living-room lamps: We shift them around to satisfy our whims or latest decorating scheme. More pragmatically, we may need to move containers into a protected area for the winter. The lighter the soil mix, the easier moving the containers will be on our backs.

Moisture retention is another important quality of container soil. Given their exposure to wind and sun, containers lose moisture much more quickly than garden soil. A container mix with a high organic content will absorb and hold water much better than a very sandy soil. Pots have to be irrigated regularly, of course, but the proper soil mix will extend the time between waterings as long as possible.

Nutrition is another consideration with container soil. The frequent watering that is so much a part of container rose gardening tends to leach nutrients, particularly nitrogen, from the soil. To compensate, plant foods need to be added regularly to the container. Some research suggests that plants fed with liquid fertilizers, which can be quickly assimilated, thrive in soils that are slightly more acidic than the soil the plant would prefer in the garden. Container soil, then, needs to be easily adaptable to the specific acid requirements of your plants.

MIXING OR BUYING SOIL

GIVEN THE DIVERSE QUALITIES OF A good container soil, the easiest way to get a properly blended batch may be to buy it. That is what I do at our nursery. Most garden centers carry artificial soils composed primarily of peat moss mixed with such materials as perlite, sand, bark or compost. The ingredients are blended by the manufacturer to meet the specific needs of your container-grown roses. All you have to do is concentrate on caring for the plants.

Many gardeners, however, prefer to mix their own soils, motivated by economics or a do-it-yourself ethic. Here is one recipe for a container mix:

In a wheelbarrow or other large container, combine 3 cubic feet of peat moss, 1 cubic foot of perlite (a whitish, water-adsorbing material derived from volcanic deposits), 3 teaspoons of superphosphate, 3 tablespoons of lime and 4 tablespoons of a balanced fertilizer such as a 10-10-10. Mix the lime thoroughly into the peat moss.

By itself, peat moss is too acidic for roses. Lime buffers the acid and raises the pH of the peat moss. Because it takes several weeks for lime to begin mitigating the acidity of the peat, mixing the lime in well in advance will provide time for the soil to "sweeten" before you are ready to use it.

We have found that adding sharp sand in an amount equal to about 10 percent of the soil volume improves drainage, compared with a straight peat moss and perlite combination, and it also adds enough weight to give small containers more stability.

Some gardeners prefer vermiculite to perlite as a constituent for improving moisture retention. Vermiculite is derived from brownish gray mica that has been rapidly heated until it expands into a spongy, absorbent

---

Pots of less than 3 gallons dry out quickly and must be watered once or twice a day.

material. I have found that artificial soils with perlite last longer and can be used for several years, while vermiculite tends to collapse and lose its water-retentive quality after a season. Your choice of vermiculite or perlite may depend on how long you plan to use the soil. Many of our roses stay in the same pot for three years. When I repot them, I use fresh soil.

FILLING THE CONTAINER

WHILE FILLING A CONTAINER WITH soil may seem ridiculously basic, there are two points worthy of discussion. One is the level of the soil. Fill the container so the soil is about 1½ inches below the rim (measure the first few pots to get a feel for the distance). This will allow enough space for watering. If you put in too much soil, water will run off before it soaks in, while too little soil leaves no room for root growth.

Second, fill the pot exclusively with soil mix. Many gardening books advise putting a layer of stones or clay shards at the bottom of a container to "improve drainage." While this advice has been repeated for years, it is inaccurate and contradicts the realities of water movement through soils. Water slows down when it hits a layer of material different from what it is moving through. This creates a wet zone where the materials change. Rather than improving drainage, a layer of stones impedes drainage and creates a swampy, oxygen-deprived area inhospitable to tender roots.

PLANTING

I PLANT CONTAINER ROSES WITH THE bud union at or just above the soil level. This makes it easier to accommodate a bush in a reasonably sized pot. Winter hardiness is not a concern, because when cold weather descends, I wrap the pot in insulating material and store it in a protected area.

Planting with the bud union above the soil level also allows me to evaluate the rose very early in the spring. If for some reason the rose has died, I can replace it, and so set out a healthy crop of container plants to ensure early and continuous flowering.

The roots on many roses I plant stretch wider than the diameter of the pot. I bend them to fit the container, and this has never seemed to harm their growth. They bloom well all summer.

I try to place the rose stalk in the center of the pot. Given the lopsided nature of most rose roots, this may not be possible in a small container, but avoid the temptation to root prune. Instead, try to bend the roots to center the stalk. If bending does not work, buy another rose or accept an offset arrangement. Planting annuals of one or more variety at the base of the rose will help disguise its off-center appearance. Choose bedding plants that complement the color of the rose. Ivies and other trailing plants can add another dimension to the design and enhance the overall appearance of the container.

PROPER WATERING

NUMEROUS RESEARCH PROJECTS have shown that adequate water can double the growth of plants in a year, compared with plants that are even slightly water deprived. Adequate moisture is particularly important to large-flowering roses. If a plant wilts, its flower buds will suffer first. Because of rapid evaporation, container-grown roses are more challenging to water than roses growing in the garden. The pots must be watered more often, and they must be watered more *slowly*, until water is freely flowing

out the bottom of the pot or hanging basket. At least 15 percent of the water should flow out at *every watering*. Flushing the container ensures that there are no dry spots to stress developing roots. Roots must be able to thrive in all parts of the soil ball, not just the top few inches moistened by shallow watering. Thorough wetting also flushes dissolved fertilizer salts from the soil, eliminating a possibly toxic buildup.

One vexing problem with peat moss soils is that if they dry out, they shrink and leave a space around the edge of the container. Irrigation water will then run down the inside of the pot and out the bottom without ever soaking into the root ball. Rehydrating the soil usually requires setting the container in a saucer or pail of water for an hour or more, depending on the size of the container. Without a thorough rewetting, the soil will be like a dry sponge, impermeable to water when you irrigate.

To avoid disturbing tender roots or digging holes in the soil when you water, fit the end of the hose with a "breaker" nozzle. The breaker will split the water into fine streams that are less likely to dig craters in the potting mix. We have found that a Dram Model 400 breaker produces the gentlest stream, and is the industry standard for most container irrigation.

How often to water is a matter of the size of the plant, the type of soil, the capacity of the container and its exposure to sun and wind. Water when the soil is dry to the touch. This may be once or twice a day for small pots or every few days for really large ones. There is no substitute for finger-touch gardening—

the touch test is the most important sense you can develop with regard to container watering. If the soil is evenly moist, the plant's growth will be even as well.

FEEDING

CONTAINER-GROWN ROSES NEED TO be fed regularly because nutrients are constantly washed out of the pots through frequent irrigation. One of the best sources of nutrients is slow-release fertilizer pellets or sticks. These are sold in a variety of strengths and differ in the length of their release time. The most common pellet is a 100-day type that releases a 14-14-14 blend of nitrogen, phosphorus and potassium. The rose receives fertilizer over the 100 days, without any additional attention from the gardener, provided the containers are regularly watered.

I have found that 2 tablespoons of pellets (a small handful) for each rose in a roughly 6-gallon pot can be just about right for the entire season. Smaller or larger pots will require different amounts. Instructions are found on the fertilizer container. Work the pellets into the top inch or so of soil.

While sticks and pellets work well for the absentminded among us, they are expensive and their release time varies, depending on how much water the plants receive. During very hot summers, roses need extra water, so the fertilizer releases very quickly, possibly leaving the plant without nutrients later in the season.

Liquid fertilizer is another option. I use a liquid feed with a 20-20-20 formulation during the summer. At every watering, plant food is applied at the appropriate rate. The roses are being fed even as older nutrients are washed out of the bottom of the container.

I am often asked whether the type of plant food matters. My answer is simple: Any food is better than no food, and the "best" plant food depends largely on the soil mix and what is most convenient for the gardener. Whatever you use, follow the directions.

One additional concern when feeding container-grown roses is that soilless mixes do not have the minor, or micro-, nutrients needed for good flowering. Check the label on your fertilizer to see whether it contains such micronutrients as iron, zinc, magnesium, calcium or copper. If these are not included, water with either a compost tea or—my favorite—a fish food fertilizer on a weekly basis. These liquids provide micronutrients in a soluble form that the plants can immediately use for the production of blossoms. Compost tea is easily made by soaking a bag of fresh compost in a bucket of water until the water turns brown. (See Chapter One, page 25, for detailed instructions on making compost and manure teas.) Fish food fertilizer is available in most garden centers.

Compost or manure teas or fish food can be used as the sole feeding program for container-grown roses. The resulting growth will be good if the fertilizer is regularly applied. We give our roses about 3 gallons a week of freshly brewed compost tea, or weekly feedings of fish food fertilizer at the manufacturer's recommended rate.

One of our current experiments indicates that a combination of long-term fertilizer pellets applied at half the recommended rate, combined with a compost tea, fish food or soluble nitrogen, also applied at half the recommended rate, produces roses of exceptional vigor and beauty. If you have the time to try this feeding regimen, I think you will be enthusiastic about the results.

PRUNING

A S WITH GARDEN ROSES, STRUCTURAL pruning of container-grown roses should be undertaken in the fall or spring, when the plant is dormant. Remove dead canes and prune off the older cane in any pair of rubbing or crossing canes. Cut hybrid teas back to 12 to 18 inches for winter storage. Prune tender climbing varieties such as 'Blaze' to encourage second-year growth. This is similar to the year three and four pruning of hardy climbers shown on page 48.

Again, as with garden roses, summer pruning is limited to removing spent flowers and pruning off flower stems. Ideally, cut the stems back to about ¼ inch above an outward-facing bud.

Root pruning, which is rarely appropriate for garden roses, can be particularly damaging to container plants. Rose roots can bend but should not be broken or cut. If you ever find yourself contemplating cutting off some roots to fit a rosebush into a particular container, put down the pruners and look for a larger pot instead. Roses have already lost most of their root structure in the harvesting process at the nursery. If the pot is too small to contain a generous root ball, it is too small to grow a plant to maturity and support the blossoms you want to see.

WINTERING

W INTERING CONTAINER PLANTS OF any kind is fraught with problems for the gardener and, indeed, even the professional nursery grower. Following a few simple rules will ensure that each plant has an excellent chance of making it through the long cold season.

First, make certain the plant is well hardened off before putting it in storage. Second, create a secure storage place and make sure your approach is well thought out.

Container roses should be dormant before they are put in storage. Dormancy is a complex physiological response to a number of conditions. Gardeners can help promote the process with a few simple steps. Stop fertilizing about mid-August or just before the third flush of blooms. Lacking fertilizer, the plant's growth slows down and the canes will begin to harden off. Some garden books advise reduced watering, but I have not found this tactic to be useful. I continue to water until the final stages of storage. Watering flushes out excess fertilizer and aids the hardening-off process. Using the "touch system," the gardener's fingers will notice that roses consume less water in the fall than in the spring and summer. Watering can be less frequent but should remain regular.

I leave our roses outside through the fall until all or most of their foliage is gone and the top of the soil has been frosted several times. The cold drives the rose into dormancy. If a rose is put into storage before it is fully dormant, it begins to consume the starches stored in its roots, the food that it relies on to support

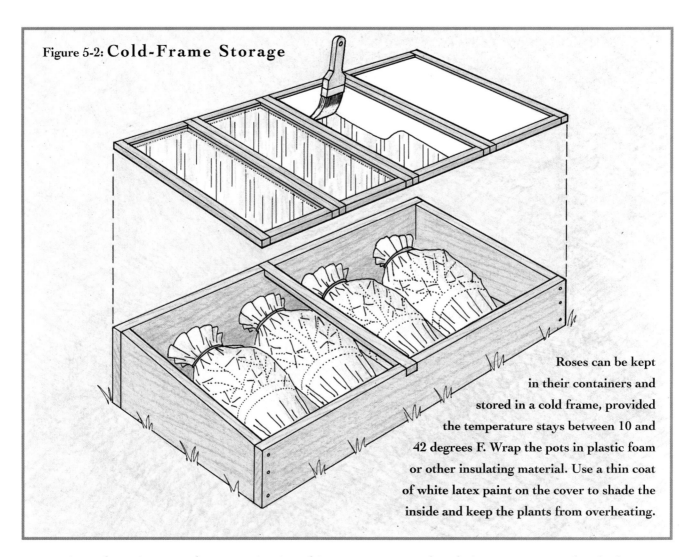

Figure 5-2: Cold-Frame Storage

Roses can be kept in their containers and stored in a cold frame, provided the temperature stays between 10 and 42 degrees F. Wrap the pots in plastic foam or other insulating material. Use a thin coat of white latex paint on the cover to shade the inside and keep the plants from overheating.

its early spring growth. By tapping into this food supply too soon, the rose's chances for survival decline.

After harvesting or deadheading the last flush of blooms, likely from the end of August to mid-September, do no further pruning until the plant is dormant. Pruning stimulates new growth, which the gardener wants to discourage at this time of year. New shoots may emerge as a result of pruning off the last flowers, but if the fertilizer is stopped, these shoots will not grow strongly. I have always ignored new growth produced by the plant at the end of the season, although some gardeners rub the shoots off as they begin to

sprout. Both techniques seem to work; which one you follow may be a matter of preference.

STORAGE OPTIONS

ONCE A ROSE IS DORMANT, GARDENERS have several storage options. The rose can be stored either in or out of the container and it can be set in the ground or kept above ground.

In the Container

If the rose is left in its container, it can be stored above ground or buried. If the choice is to store it above ground, several conditions should be met. It is useful to understand that many roots die when their temperature falls to 5 degrees F. Some roots are hardier than others, but the 5 degree rule is widely applicable. At the same time, rose roots need to be kept cool. If storage temperatures go above 50 degrees F for several days in a row, the plant will begin to break dormancy.

At our gardens and nursery, I keep most of our large container plants, such as roses and fruit trees, in a cold frame in which the temperature is not allowed to go below 10 degrees F or above 42 degrees F for the entire winter (Figure 5-2). Any location that stays a relatively uniform temperature between these two points, such as an unheated basement or a garage, will be fine for storing container roses.

During storage, the soil in a container should not be allowed to dry out. Although the plant is dormant, the roots will die without water. Normally, if the temperature is cool enough, a single watering in January or February is enough to keep the soil damp through the winter. Check the soil moisture monthly using the touch test, and water only when your fingers tell you it is time.

Covering the container with an insulating blanket can improve its chances for survival. Some handy gardeners construct boxes lined with plastic foam insulation to protect their plants. Some wrap their roses with old quilts or blankets.

At our gardens, I use polyfoam, a flexible plastic foam that you may be able to find at your local garden center. If you can't locate it, it's worth hunting for. If there is a small plant nursery near your home, you may be able to buy some polyfoam from the owner.

One material that is *not* appropriate for winter covering is airtight plastic wrap. Besides being of little insulating value, plastic does not allow any air exchange or evaporation, and it traps heat, which can lead to premature budding and kill the plant. A sealed environment also contributes to the growth of fungal spores in the soil.

No covering, however, will totally insulate container-grown plants from the ravages of winter. In most cases, the plants need shelter as well. Wrapping and leaving a plant outside will only result in a dead rose. What wrapping *can* do, in conjunction with some shelter, is moderate temperature extremes and protect roses from rapid fluctuations in temperature.

An exception to the poor prognosis for unsheltered plants may be found on urban balconies (Figure 5-3, page 96). If a well-wrapped group of plants is stored against a glass door or window, there will be enough warmth to ease them through the winter, provided they are shielded from the drying effect of the wind and have plenty of insulation under the containers. Balcony conditions are not as benevolent as indoor storage, but if you make the best of what you have, the roses may well live to bloom again.

If you garden outside the city and have neither a cold frame, unheated garage nor root cellar, try this old nursery technique (Figure 5-4, page 97): After the plants are dormant and the pots have been frosted several times, water the soil well and lay the containers on their sides on the ground. Pack the pots together tightly. The woody tops will mingle

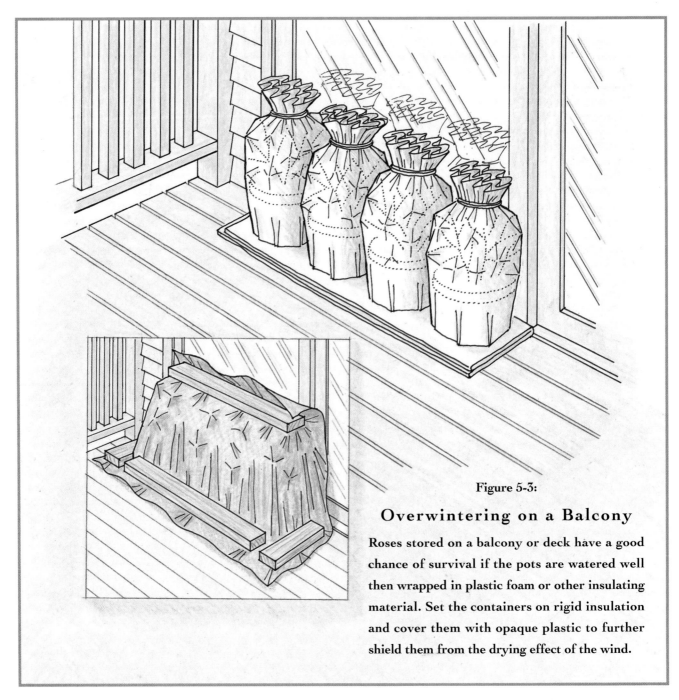

Figure 5-3:

Overwintering on a Balcony

Roses stored on a balcony or deck have a good chance of survival if the pots are watered well then wrapped in plastic foam or other insulating material. Set the containers on rigid insulation and cover them with opaque plastic to further shield them from the drying effect of the wind.

and the branches may bend, but this can be safely ignored and the damage repaired in the spring with judicious pruning. What is most important is getting the pots close enough together to act as a single insulating mass. Liberally apply waterproof mouse bait, found at most hardware stores, around the plants, then make a winter quilt.

Use white nursery plastic for the base of the quilt. Clear plastic will allow too much heat to build up, while black plastic will screen out too much light. The sheet of white plastic should be large enough so that half of it will cover all the plants. Pull half the sheet over the containers, then cover the mound with 2 feet of loose straw, enough to bring

Figure 5-4: Outdoor Storage

Container roses can be stored outdoors
using an old nursery technique.

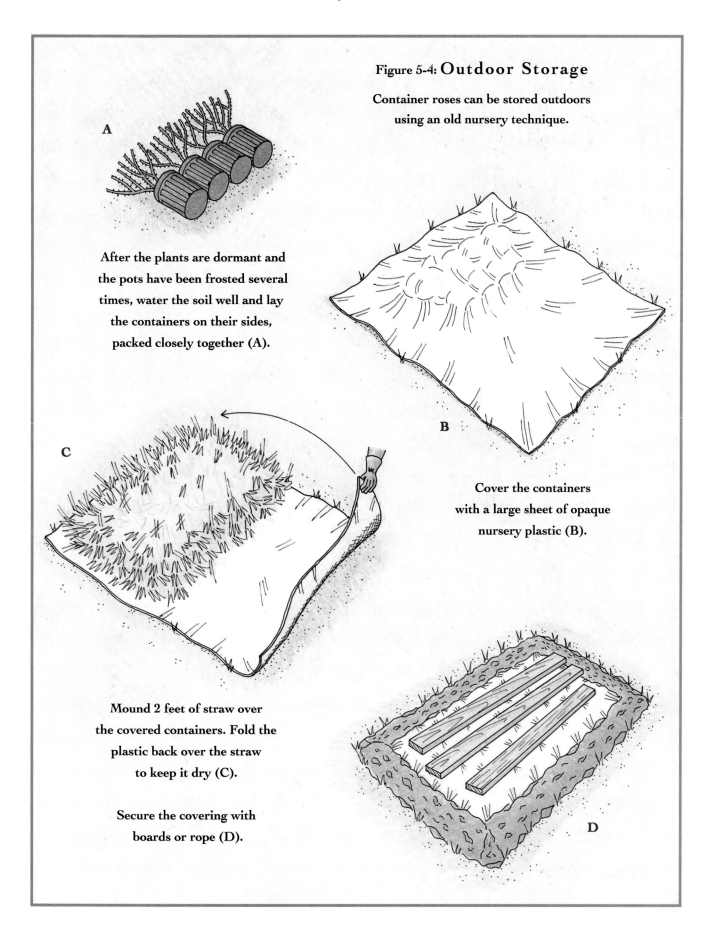

A

After the plants are dormant and
the pots have been frosted several
times, water the soil well and lay
the containers on their sides,
packed closely together (A).

B

Cover the containers
with a large sheet of opaque
nursery plastic (B).

C

Mound 2 feet of straw over
the covered containers. Fold the
plastic back over the straw
to keep it dry (C).

Secure the covering with
boards or rope (D).

D

Figure 5-5: **Burying a Rose out of its Container**

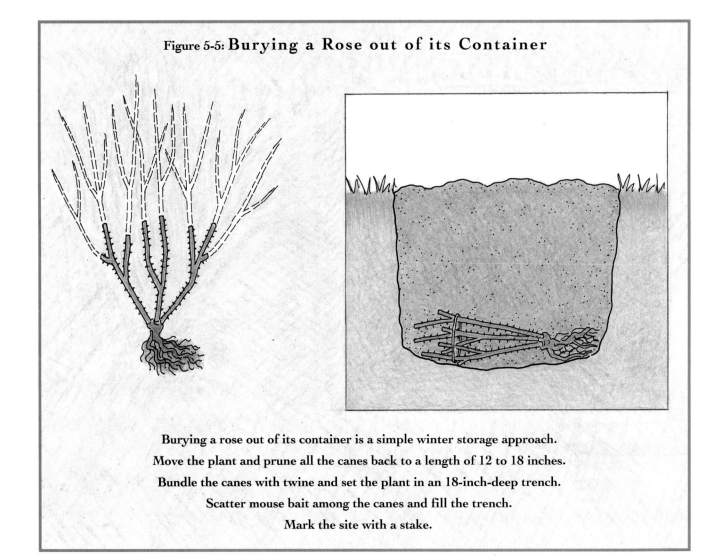

Burying a rose out of its container is a simple winter storage approach.
Move the plant and prune all the canes back to a length of 12 to 18 inches.
Bundle the canes with twine and set the plant in an 18-inch-deep trench.
Scatter mouse bait among the canes and fill the trench.
Mark the site with a stake.

most containerized roses through a cold winter. Pull the rest of the plastic over the straw to keep it dry. Bury the edges of the plastic to keep out wandering rodents and winter breezes. You may need to anchor the mound with ropes or boards to keep it in place. If the straw is kept dry, the blanket system works about as well as any more expensive and sophisticated shelter.

Remove the blanket in the spring as daytime temperatures begin to climb and after nighttime temperatures are consistently above 5 degrees F. In our Zone 4 garden, I uncover outside stored plants during the last

week of March. Gardeners can delay this date by a week for every zone colder than 4 or advance it a week for every zone warmer than 4.

Once plants are uncovered, set them upright and water them thoroughly. Prune off rodent-damaged branches, but delay general pruning for several weeks to give the plants time to straighten themselves naturally.

This method of winter storage went out of fashion commercially because it is so labor intensive. Moving mountains of straw can be unpleasant and time consuming. On a small scale, however, the work is manageable, and the straw can be composted or used as mulch in the vegetable garden. Dry leaves, if you can pile them deeply enough, are a good substitute for straw. Peat moss is too opaque and dense, while hay introduces weed seeds wherever you pile it.

Out of the Container

Storing a rose in the container below ground means digging a trench large enough to bury the plant *and* the pot. This is a lot of work. It is easier to take the rose out of the container, store the container in the shed and bury the plant by itself (Figure 5-5).

Here is one approach for underground storage: Remove the rose from its container and prune all the canes back to 12 to 18 inches. Leave the roots unpruned. If you are working with climbing roses, leave them unpruned as well. Merely bundle them together with twine to form a tight column.

Dig a trench 18 inches deep and long enough to comfortably accommodate the plant. Lay the rose lengthwise in the trench, scatter some weatherproof mouse bait around the canes and refill the trench. Put a marking stick on the trench to help you find the roses in the spring.

The ground should be almost frozen when you put the roses in the trench. An inch or two of frost in the ground is not a hazard to the roses; it hopefully means that the mice will have already settled in elsewhere and will not be searching for rose canes as winter food. In our Zone 4 garden, the first week of November is the perfect time to bury roses, as either there is already an inch of frost in the ground or there will be within a few days. Gardeners can delay burying by a week for every zone warmer than Zone 4, or advance the date by a week for every zone colder than Zone 4.

I grow roses in containers for several reasons. I like to see blooming roses in various, sometimes surprising, places in the landscape. And I like to keep the design changing. It is a lot easier to move a pot than to dig a garden every time I want to look at a rose in a new spot. Container roses are punctuation marks in the garden, drawing particular attention and admiration from visitors.

But the most rewarding reason for my growing container roses is personal. When I sit down for tea after a day's work in the nursery and savor that first warm sip, I can inhale the fragrance of the roses growing in their containers close by and feel that my horticultural efforts have been worthwhile.

Chapter Six

PEST *and* DISEASE PRIMER

R OSES SUFFER FROM BAD PRESS. THE COMMON story is that they are disease-ridden plants that the average gardener is unable to grow. They are said to be hard to overwinter and to rarely return enough flowers or fragrance to justify the cost and effort.

It is true that our roses are from time to time troubled by pests and disease. But on the whole, they are healthy, attractive, undemanding plants, well worth the small bit of work they require.

The key to growing healthy roses is to keep them free of stress. This cannot be overstated. Timely feeding, watering and pruning is the best preventive management you can provide. Routine care saves time. It spares you the need for major renovations and

Damage from black spot (above) and Japanese beetles (left) can be reduced by good management.

reduces your reliance on chemicals and other disease controls to try to restore your roses' health. Prevention is more certain than cure.

That said, I'll admit that I have lowered my expectations a bit as well. I accept that my plants may be hit with some black spot by August. I also know that aphids and other insects are likely to descend on my plants. I don't panic. I understand that these things are part of the regular cycle of our garden, and I am prepared to use a number of practices to discourage them.

The foundation of my management strategy is good soil fertility, combined with environmentally sensitive disease and pest controls. I rarely spray our roses in anticipation that they *might* be troubled by insects or disease; I reserve spraying for problems that I can actually identify. Some years I do not spray at all, while in other years I may use a small amount of organic fungicide or pesticide to help the plants resist encroaching diseases or pests.

Black spot is one disease I sometimes target for special treatment, because it can be quite destructive to many rose varieties. If, for some reason, I have a particularly bad year, I may resort to some preventive spraying the following year to try to keep the disease in check.

My relaxed attitude about insects and diseases and the following organic practices have kept our gardens thriving and made them enjoyable places to work and visit. Experience has shown me that organic methods are, for the most part, as successful as any chemical approach. If organic methods are appropriate for our garden and nursery business, they will work for the average home gardener who is tending many fewer plants.

DISEASES

Black Spot

The primary disease concern for most rose growers is the fungal ailment black spot (*Diplocarpon rosae*). Black spot occurs in almost all rose gardens sooner or later and initially causes a dime-size black spot on the leaf, a spot that grows as the disease spreads. Unlike some other diseases that appear only on the top or bottom of a leaf, black spot can occur on either side.

Identifying black spot is relatively easy using a magnifying glass. If the edges of the circle are smooth, the ailment is probably common leaf spot. If the edges are fringed like a drop of ink on white paper, the disease is almost certainly black spot.

While many mildew or fungus problems confine themselves to the surface of a leaf, black spot puts its threads, or mycelium, under the leaf surface into the cuticle, or upper cell layer. In getting below the surface, the organism protects itself from most fungicides. Once established, black spot is almost impossible to eradicate with sprays. In time, infected leaves fall off, either from stress, from the progression of the fungus or from the fungal production of ethylene gas. Defoliation of the entire cane can happen quickly if the disease is left unchecked. The loss of foliage weakens a rose. It diminishes its food-gathering ability, causing poor blossom production and lowering its chances for winter survival.

What is a gardener to do when faced with such a prevalent and canny disease? As with many diseases, there is not one simple response that will eradicate the problem. However, there are several steps, combining plant selection and care, that can keep it in check.

To begin with, some roses are resistant to black spot. Garden centers and mail-order companies should be familiar with these varieties. Resistant plants are not immune to black spot, but they resist its onset until late in the season, when it will be confined to a few leaves and cause little damage.

Beyond choosing resistant varieties, gardeners can employ a number of horticultural techniques and selective spraying programs to discourage the disease.

Unlike many rose gardeners, I rarely use preventive sprays. I do not want a fungus or bacteria constantly exposed to any pesticide because, invariably, a mutant strain will develop with resistance to the spray. But if I have a severe infestation of black spot one year, I often spray my most susceptible roses the next year, before the disease is evident. I've found that a few well-timed sprays early in the season either eliminate the disease or reduce its damage to a negligible level.

The two sprays I use are lime-sulfur and baking soda, and I alternate their application so that the fungus is less likely to develop resistance to either one. I make an initial application of dormant oil and lime-sulfur on a warm, sunny spring day, while the canes are still dormant and before the buds are beginning to swell. The spray can prevent young spores of black spot from becoming established, and it will kill other overwintering fungal and mildew problems as well. Later in the season, when the leaves are open, I thoroughly cover all plant surfaces with lime-sulfur. Some conventional rose growers, raising highly susceptible varieties, spray their plants once a week throughout the season and after every rain.

Baking soda, or sodium bicarbonate, is our other black spot spray. An alkaline substance, baking soda prevents spores from colonizing and kills young infestations, apparently by raising the pH of the leaf surface. I mix 2 teaspoons of baking soda with 1 gallon of lukewarm water and add 1 tablespoon of either insecticidal soap or dish soap to help the spray spread evenly and adhere to leaf surfaces. I mix the ingredients thoroughly and use the spray immediately. I mix up a fresh batch each time I spray.

For severe black spot infestations, rotate baking soda and lime-sulfur spray every five to seven days and after a rain. While the sprays will not destroy established spores, they will protect uninfected leaves.

More important than spraying, in protecting our roses from black spot, is our horticultural approach. If the fungus is allowed to overwinter on fallen leaves or standing canes, it will send out new colonizing spores in the spring. As part of our deep planting system, I prune off the aboveground canes from our cold-tender hybrid roses in the fall and rake up the foliage from all our shrub and climbing plants, thereby eliminating the habitat for the fungus. I do not compost this debris; instead, I burn it. If burning is not practical, you might dispose of the plant material in your trash.

If you live in an area with mild winters or if you hill your roses, the canes will survive. Pruning these canes in the spring to within a few inches of the bud union will reduce the incidence of black spot more than any other practice, according to studies by the U.S. Department of Agriculture. Our deep planting method and the removal of canes in the fall limits the appearance of black spot to late in the season.

Mulching, too, keeps black spot at bay. Mulching prevents water from splashing up around plants and helps to keep the leaves dry. This discourages the fungus from spreading, because it needs moisture to thrive. I have long been an advocate of mulching for weed control, fertility, retaining moisture and moderating soil temperatures, but in the rose beds, the greatest benefit of mulch may be in suppressing black spot.

Do not allow infested rose leaves to lie on the garden soil for any length of time. Once they have fallen, pick them up and dispose of them out of the garden.

Some gardeners report that planting garlic and onions at the base of roses deters black spot fungus. I am still experimenting with this companion-planting approach and would recommend only that other gardeners do the same.

Powdery Mildew

Primary symptoms of powdery mildew (*Sphaerotheca pannosa* var. *rosae*) include curling leaves or leaves that develop a purplish cast. The white film that characterizes powdery mildew on many plants such as garden phlox or lilacs is not as evident on roses, but the impact of the disease is quite apparent. Infected leaves may be found as far down the canes as 18 inches from the tips. The ends of seriously infected canes will die and the flower buds will not open.

Prune out diseased canes as soon as you notice them, and clean up any leaf and cane residue from around your plants each fall. Otherwise, powdery mildew will overwinter in the plant debris.

As with black spot, a spray of lime-sulfur in the spring, while the rose is dormant, will knock back any overwintering spores on the surviving canes. A second application in late April or May when the buds are swelling can help control an early-season outbreak. If the plant is infected with powdery mildew during the flowering season, prune off all diseased leaves and canes, and apply either lime-sulfur or baking soda. (See page 103 for directions for mixing a baking soda spray.) Rotate applications of lime-sulfur and baking soda, putting on one or the other every seven to ten days, if powdery mildew continues to plague your plants.

Botrytis Blight

One of the most frustrating experiences in rose gardening is watching as a plant's large developing buds turn brown and decay. Sometimes, even buds that are partially open and showing color will start to brown and shrivel. The cause, invariably, is botrytis blight (*Botrytis cinerea*). One of the most common fungi on earth, botrytis thrives in rainy weather, when leaves and blossoms stay damp for several days. Even routinely wetting rose leaves when watering plants invites this fungus.

Botrytis can be combated with a lime-sulfur spray applied early in the spring while rose plants are still dormant. If the blight appears later in the season, use a lime-sulfur or a baking soda spray and rotate the sprays, apply-

Canes afflicted with powdery mildew should be pruned off and removed from the garden.

ing one or the other every seven to ten days and after a rain. (See the recipe for mixing baking soda spray, page 103.)

White-flowering roses are more susceptible to botrytis than red-flowering ones, but no matter what color your roses, picking off all old, faded blooms will help to control the establishment or spread of this disease. Botrytis spores survive the winter on decaying leaves and old stems. Removing plant debris, especially at the end of the season, is an excellent preventive practice.

Cankers

Cankers are evidenced by a slightly sunken area of the cane, often with cracks radiating away from the depression. While the pattern of the cracks provides some indication of the specific type of canker, the treatment is the same for all variants: Prune off and destroy the afflicted canes. Remove these cuttings from the garden, but do not compost them.

There is some research to suggest that canes that have been hilled for the winter, especially those hilled with oak, maple or other tree leaves, are more likely to contract canker than unprotected canes. Our very low incidence of canker on cold-tender roses may be explained by the deep planting method, in which I prune off all aboveground canes in the fall.

Once canes are infected with canker, there is no spray that will eliminate it. The canes must be pruned off. As a follow-up, you can apply a lime-sulfur or a baking soda spray to help prevent a recurrence. (See page 103 for instructions on mixing a baking soda spray.)

PESTS

Aphids

Four species of aphids can be found on roses: green peach (*Myzus persicae*), melon (*Aphis gossypii*), potato (*Macrosiphum euphorbiae*) and rose aphid (*Macrosiphum rosae*). These pests are small pear-shaped creatures that appear in great numbers on the rose cane tips in May and early June. While sometimes the young brood have a pink cast, or the odd one is black, the majority are a lime-green. They multiply extremely rapidly, suddenly appearing in such great numbers that it seems as if a huge migration has arrived overnight.

Aphids congregate primarily on the tender tips of rose canes, but they can also be found hiding under the leaves in search of food. They eat away at the growing tips and leaves to suck out the juice. The foliage becomes distorted and eventually curls up, turns yellow and dies. The shoot tips will also die under severe infestations. Not only do aphids disfigure roses, they carry diseases, moving viruses and bacteria from infected to healthy plants. What's more, aphids excrete a dark, sticky substance called "honeydew," which is consumed by ants. The ants, in turn, move the aphids to less-populated leaves, treating them, in effect, as prized livestock for food production.

In our gardens, there is a spring explosion of aphids on roses and several other flowering plants, and I use a variety of approaches to control them. Probably the fastest, easiest way is squeezing them with my fingers and knocking them off the canes or washing down infested plants with a brisk spray from the

Aphids congregate primarily on the buds and tender tips of rose canes.

hose. Some research indicates that once sprayed off, aphids do not find their way back to the canes and recolonize.

I have also used insecticidal soap sprayed on infested canes and foliage. The soap does not leave any residual toxicity that would harm beneficial insects. However, it must be reapplied every day or two until the infestation is reduced. Rotenone, applied either as a dust or as a wettable powder spray, also works well, as do pyrethrum-based sprays.

Some gardeners employ diatomaceous earth for aphid control, although the approaches mentioned above are probably more effective. Diatomaceous earth is a powder made from the fossilized remains of tiny sea creatures called diatoms. One of its attractive qualities is that, unless it is inhaled, it is harmless to humans and pets, while to soft-bodied insects it is razor sharp and tears their exterior casing. Diatomaceous earth easily washes off leaves and canes and must be reapplied after a rain.

Adult ladybird beetles and larvae consume large quantities of aphids. Some gardeners buy hundreds of adult beetles, then release them in their rose or vegetable beds. Unfortunately, the insects do not recognize geographic boundaries and have no allegiance to their purchaser. There is no way to prevent them from suddenly, inexplicably, dispersing to neighboring yards. Perhaps—and I mention this with my tongue firmly in my cheek— you might release the beetles in your neighbor's garden in hopes that they eventually land in yours. Otherwise, it is probably best to rely on the natural population.

When I use sprays on aphids or any other insects, I alternate materials. If I use insecticidal soap initially, I follow up with rotenone. Then I use pyrethrum before spraying soap again. Rotating controls keeps the insects from developing resistance to a particular toxin. If a spray is used exclusively and regularly, the insects that survive live to breed and pass on their resistance, creating an ever-larger resistant population.

Once the spring outbreak of aphids has been reduced, I rarely have another damaging infestation. Aphids are certainly present, but I don't resort to sprays, as natural predators tend to keep the population in check. Ladybird beetles, wasps, predatory mites and hummingbirds visit our plants regularly and provide a balance that allows the roses to bloom free of toxic sprays.

Caterpillars

Every spring, about the time the first flower buds appear, our roses are infested with small caterpillars or loopers that chew up quite a few leaves in a surprisingly short time. If not dispatched quickly, they will move up the plant, sampling leaves until they arrive at the buds, which they will bore through to reach the soft tissue of the flower. Most of the time these small engines of devastation are a soft green color that allows them to nestle inconspicuously in the rose foliage. To find them, examine the edge of a leaf. Because they rarely stop eating long enough to move, they are easily spotted at the point of damage.

Caterpillar control is quite easy. The fastest and surest way is to squeeze them between your fingers. You'll use no sprays, no dusts and have instant results. If you are squeamish about squashing, wearing gloves might make the job less offensive.

Spraying caterpillars with water does *not* help. The caterpillars merely climb back on the nearest rosebush and resume lunch.

Rotenone, pyrethrum and diatomaceous earth work well against caterpillars, as does the bacterium *Bacillus thuringiensis.* Bt, as it is known, kills caterpillars and loopers without harming nontarget pests, but it does not kill them right away. Once a caterpillar eats Bt, it stops feeding and usually dies a few days later. Bt is available in the United States but not in Canada.

Controlling caterpillars as soon as you notice leaf damage is the best way to keep their numbers in check. It is not important to identify the particular caterpillar inhabiting your roses, because the controls are the same for all of them. One strategy that should be ongoing year to year is a thorough cleaning of the rose beds each fall. Because caterpillars overwinter on garden debris, removing their habitat reduces the likelihood of an infestation in the spring.

Cane Borer

Cane borers (*Aberea maculata*) feed as readily on roses as on raspberries. The injury and the controls are similar for both plants. The borer attacks canes 6 to 8 inches from their tip, causing the cane to wilt and droop. Because the larvae are feeding inside the cane, no sprays or dusts will work on them. Simply cut the cane off several inches below the infestation marks: two parallel lines ½ to 1 inch apart, around the cane. Often there is a slightly raised

or discolored section between the marks.

After cutting, inspect the end of the remaining cane to make sure it is smooth. If it is hollowed out, the larvae are still active lower in the stem. Prune again until the top is smooth. Do not compost the prunings. Instead, burn them or put them in the trash.

Earwigs

I am often asked if earwigs (*Forficula auricularia*) bother my garden, and my answer is always "No." These reddish brown ¾-inch-long rear-pincered pests are in the garden, to be sure, because when digging through my mulched beds, I often see them scurrying away from the trowel or spade. But I rarely see any damage—such as chewed-off blossoms or leaves—that can be blamed on these creatures. I believe my lack of problems is due to heavy mulching. A mulched garden gives the earwigs both food and a place to hide, and I believe they prefer to eat and hide rather than expose themselves high up on a rose blossom.

If gardeners prefer not to mulch, applying a dusting of diatomaceous earth to bottom leaves and lower canes will discourage earwigs from climbing up the plants to reach the flower buds. After walking through the dust, earwigs will stop to groom and ingest some of the sharp shards. Diatomaceous earth washes off easily, so plants need to be dusted again after a rain.

Another, more complicated, approach involves setting 1-foot sections of ¾-inch-diameter pipe around the garden. The earwigs are apt to hide in the pipe during the day. If you tap out the pipes into a bucket of soapy water or kerosene, you will keep the earwig population down. Similarly, earwigs will take refuge under boards laid among the rosebushes. You can turn the boards over and squash the earwigs to achieve a certain measure of population control.

Leaf Rollers

Leaf rollers have never been a major problem for our rosebushes, but occasionally one will decide to take up residence. The caterpillar involved, usually the oblique-banded leaf roller (*Choristoneura rosaceana*), is pale green with a black head, and it often eats leaves and chews holes in flower buds. For protection, it rolls a leaf around itself, then glues the edges together with strands of silk. The rolled leaves wither and die. While there are several types of leaf rollers, the controls are the same for all of them.

Spraying is pointless because the caterpillar is wrapped inside the leaf. The only solution is to cut off the leaf or squeeze it to kill the caterpillar. Normally, because the leaf roller always picks the choicest, youngest foliage, I'll squeeze the leaf tube to kill the pest, then unwrap it to allow the leaf to continue growing.

Dormant oil sprays will reduce leaf roller populations on shrub roses or exposed canes that survive the winter. A fungicide such as lime-sulfur can be added to dormant oil spray for an early-spring application that will deter not only leaf rollers but black spot and other fungal diseases as well.

Rose Slugs

The bristly rose slug (*Cladius isomerus*) is another pale green caterpillar, distinguished from the oblique-banded leaf roller by having a brown head instead of a black one. Approximately ¾ inch long, this caterpillar skeletonizes rose leaves. If a leaf has been reduced to a lacework of veins, with the interior greenery chewed away, rose slugs are the likely culprit. Feeding at night, they are rarely seen by the gardener. An insecticide that remains toxic for several hours or—even better—a few days, such as rotenone or diatomaceous earth, is most effective against rose slugs. Apply the control to the entire plant, especially around the heavily damaged areas.

Ground Slugs

Sometimes, our old friend the garden slug will visit our roses. Crawling up the shorter hybrid tea roses, the slug will enjoy a salad of lower leaves.

While not often caught in the act, because it feeds at night, the slug leaves telltale signs of ragged foliage and a trail of slime. Some authorities suggest erecting barriers of copper strips or sinking saucers of beer to lure slugs to an alcoholic death, but I have never had much success with these techniques. Our garden design does not lend itself to barriers, and our dog drinks the beer. My approach has been to sprinkle diatomaceous earth at the base of plants, on the canes and on any leaves touching the ground.

Rose Chafer

This ½-inch-long gray beetle (*Macrodactylus subspinosus*) is a slow mover in the garden. It won't scuttle away if disturbed, and it's found on roses, on other perennials such as peonies and hollyhocks, and on grapevines.

The eggs of the beetle are laid in the

ground and the larvae feed on grass roots. The larvae can do an incredible amount of damage there, and gardeners may mistakenly identify them as the larvae of Japanese beetle. Control at this lawn stage is accomplished by the application of milky spore (*Bacillus popilliae*) or by the use of the predator nematode *Steinernema carpocapsae*. Neither of these products is pest specific; that is, each will attack a large range of similar pests.

If the larvae are allowed to hatch, the adult beetle will happily feed on roses but can be controlled with either hand picking, rotenone, pyrethrum or diatomaceous earth.

Rose Curculio

This weevil (*Rhynchites bicolor*) is unmistakable in the garden. Approximately ¼ inch long, red on the top and black underneath, it has a long snout with which it eats deep holes in rose buds. The damaged buds usually fail to open. (If you do open one, you will notice that the petals are full of holes.) Because the small white larvae of this pest feed on buds and seedpods, prompt pruning of infected buds and old rose hips is good management.

With attentive cleanup, this pest will not be a major problem in the garden. In fact, it rarely shows its snout in ours. Control of adult wee-

Japanese beetles favor buds and flowers but also feed on foliage.
They can be picked off and dropped into a container of soapy water or kerosene.

vils, should they persist, is by rotenone, pyrethrum or diatomaceous earth.

Japanese Beetle

These beetles (*Popillia japonica*) are ½ inch long, with a shiny, metallic green body and copper-colored wing covers. The larvae are 1½-inch-long white grubs with dark heads, and are found mostly in lawns. Both stages of the Japanese beetle are problems for gardeners, but only the adult stage attacks roses directly. The beetles favor buds and flowers but will turn their attention to the leaves when the more delectable parts of the plant are gone. Hungry beetles can ruin the floral display and defoliate a rosebush in a surprisingly short time. The beetles can be picked off by hand and dropped into a can of soapy water or kerosene. Applying rotenone or pyrethrum to leaves and canes will also reduce the population.

Controlling Japanese beetles at the larval stage is a good gardening practice and will preserve many blooms. The beetle lays its eggs in turf, and this is where they should be controlled. Applying predator nematodes is a short-term solution, but for long-term reduction, apply milky spore bacteria (*Bacillus popilliae*), described in detail on page 115.

Rose Leafhopper

The rose leafhopper (*Edwardsiana rosea*) is one of more than 2,000 species of leafhopper. It is a ¼-inch-long wedge-shaped greenish insect that sucks out the sap from the underside of leaves, which causes a stippling effect on the top surface that resembles the damage done by spider mites. If the insects continue to feed, leaves will wither and brown and fall from the plant. A heavy infestation causes severe defoliation.

Spraying leaves, particularly on the undersides, with insecticidal soap will discourage rose leafhoppers.

ORGANIC PEST CONTROL PRODUCTS

Insecticidal Soap

Soap sprays have proved their worth in the greenhouses and gardens at our nursery. Mixed according to the directions on the label, generally 1 part soap to 40 parts water, this spray quickly knocks down soft-bodied insects. I have experimented with soap from the kitchen and found that it, too, has a killing action similar to soaps sold as insecticides. However, the kitchen soaps (not detergents) tend to burn plants more easily than the insecticidal soaps, so they should be mixed at a weaker concentration.

Soft water with a neutral pH is very important for increasing the effectiveness of soap sprays; avoid hard and alkaline water. Gardeners may want to use rainwater, snow melt or distilled water as a carrier for the soap. Alternate with other methods of insect control, as aphids and other pests will develop resistance to soap sprays.

Some recipes call for adding 1 tablespoon of rubbing alcohol for every pint of spray solution to increase the potency of the soap spray. This is not a common practice at our nursery but might be worth trying for such hard-shelled pests as Japanese beetles.

Spraying insecticidal soap discourages aphids and other
soft-bodied pests without much threat to humans or beneficial insects.
If using a toxic spray, wear rubber gloves and a long-sleeved shirt.

Diatomaceous Earth

Made from the fossilized remains of microscopic sea creatures, diatomaceous earth feels like talcum powder to humans and their pets but is razor sharp and deadly to many insects. It cuts the skin of soft-bodied pests such as slugs, causing dehydration. Pests that groom themselves, such as earwigs, eat the shards and die from internal damage. As a powder, diatomaceous earth can be sprinkled around the base of rose canes or on leaves. It can also be mixed with water for spraying at a rate of 1 tablespoon to about 1 pint of water. The exact amount of water is not critical, as the water merely acts as a carrier to get the powder to the leaf or insect. Keep shaking the container while spraying to hold the powder in suspension. Adding 1 teaspoon of soap to this solution will act as a surfactant, allowing it to spread more easily.

Rotenone

Rotenone is an organic insecticide produced from the roots of certain tropical plants (family Lonchocarpus, plants such as *Derris*, *Barbasco* and *Timbo* species). Rotenone is a nonselective poison that disrupts the nervous systems of any creature—destructive or beneficial—that ingests or absorbs it. It will knock down just about any pest in the garden. This can be particularly satisfying if aphids are taking over the rose tips, but it can be a problem if rotenone is indiscriminately and generously used for any minor infestation. Rotenone is particularly toxic to fish, birds and pigs. It is less toxic to humans, but I never use it without wearing gloves and a dust mask.

Rotenone breaks down quickly in sunlight and loses its toxicity in less than four days. It is sold as either a dusting powder or a wettable powder for mixing with water. Use it in rotation with other insecticides rather than relying on it exclusively.

Pyrethrum

Pyrethrum is a fast-acting insecticide toxic to many garden pests. It loses its toxicity in less than eight hours once exposed to sunlight and moisture, so repeated applications may be necessary.

Pyrethrum is derived primarily from pyrethrum daisies (*Tanacetum coccineum*). Some herbalists claim that the plant *Tanacetum cinerariifolium* produces pyrethrum of a better quality. You may want to experiment, as both plants are readily available from mail-order seed companies.

Harvest the flowers just before they open and show color for the first time. Dry thoroughly, then pulverize them. Apply the powder to rose leaves and canes. Always wear a dust mask when working with pyrethrum or any other insecticide.

Pyrethrum is seldom available at local garden centers, although the synthetic form, known as pyrethrin, is sometimes carried. A manufactured product, pyrethrin has similar effects on some insects but is much longer lasting in the environment.

Predator Nematodes

The predator nematode *Steinernema carpocapsae*, sold under such trade names as BioSafe, is a naturally occurring nematode or small eelworm found in our gardens. The nematode attacks very slow moving grubs and larvae in the soil and parasitizes them. Grubs, cutworms, fungus gnats and flea larvae are among the nematode's prey. Earthworms are veritable speed demons and are not susceptible to this beneficial predator.

The service of predator nematodes is surprisingly easy to enlist in the garden. They come in their own storage medium, and when mixed with water they wake up ready to eat. The solution can be activated right in a watering can and applied to your rose beds. A package of nematodes will cover a specific area, say, 1,000 square feet. The size of the watering can is not critical—1 gallon, 2 gallons or larger. What is important is that you apply the solution evenly to the coverage area.

Follow the directions to ensure survival of as many beneficials as possible. (Having paid for them, it would be foolish to treat them badly and kill them.) As long as the soil is warm and moist, the nematodes "swim" between soil particles and attack all food sources in the area. Once the food sources, or garden pests, are eliminated, the nematode population will die back to naturally occurring levels. This means that if nematodes are applied in the early spring to fight cutworms, their population will have crashed by July and August when most grubs are hatching. For control of these late-hatching creatures, more nematodes will have to be introduced.

Milky Spore

Sold under such names as Doom, milky spore produces a bacterium (*Bacillus popilliae*) that parasitizes and kills Japanese beetle grubs. The bacteria works best in warm, slightly damp soil conditions, so don't apply milky spore early in the spring when the ground is cold. Apply the powder in very small patches 3 feet apart (a small spot is fine) in a row across the lawn. Continue making rows 3 feet apart until the lawn resembles a small checkerboard.

The spores live in the soil indefinitely but will need several years to develop enough of a population to control the grubs. The predator nematode described above can be used for short-term control.

OUR VISITORS ARE SOMETIMES AMAZED to find various insect and disease problems in the gardens of someone who not only pursues horticulture for a living but writes about it. As a professional, I have come to understand that insects and disease are part of the natural cycle. Gardeners have to coexist with these other life forms. They cannot be entirely eradicated. While we need to be vigilant to prevent an insect population or pathogen from destroying our roses, we also need to cultivate a relaxed attitude. We grow roses to enjoy their blossoms and their fragrance, not to strategize over how to defeat the pests that feed on them. Amid this hectic life we, indeed, need to take time to stop and smell the roses.

RESOURCES

**Carl Pallek and Son
Nurseries**
Box 137
Virgil, ON
Canada L0S 1T0
(905) 468-7262 (phone)
(905) 468-5246 (fax)
FREE CATALOG. DOES NOT SHIP TO
U.S.

Carroll Gardens Inc.
444 E. Main St.
Westminster, MD 21157
(410) 848-5422 (within MD)
(800) 638-6334 (outside MD)
(410) 857-4112 (fax)
CATALOG $3.

Corn Hill Nursery Ltd.
RR 5, Route 890
Petitcodiac, NB
Canada E0A 2H0
(506) 756-3635 (phone)
(506) 756-1087 (fax)
CATALOG $2.

Greenmantle Nursery
3010 Ettersburg Rd.
Garberville, CA 95542
(707) 986-7504
SPECIALIZES IN OLD AND UNUSUAL
ROSES; SEND A SASE.

**Gurney's Seed and
Nursery Co.**
110 Capital St.
Yankton, SD 57079
(605) 665-1930 (phone)
(605) 665-9718 (fax)
FREE CATALOG. DOES NOT SHIP
OUTSIDE CONTINENTAL U.S.

Heritage Rose Gardens
16831 Mitchell Creek Dr.
Fort Bragg, CA 95437
(707) 964-3748
CATALOG $2.

Historical Roses
1657 W. Jackson St.
Painesville, OH 44077
(216) 357-7270
FREE CATALOG.

Honeywood Lilies
Box 68
Parkside, SK
Canada S0J 2A0
(306) 747-3926 (phone)
(306) 747-3395 (fax)
CATALOG $2.

Hortico Inc.
723 Robson Rd.
Waterdown, ON
Canada L0R 2H1
(905) 689-6984 (phone)
(905) 689-6566 (fax)
CATALOG $3.

Lowe's Own Root Roses
6 Sheffield Rd.
Nashua, NH 03062
(603) 888-2214 (phone)
(603) 888-6112 (fax)
CATALOG $3.

Pickering Nurseries
670 Kingston Rd.
Pickering, ON
Canada L1V 1A6
(905) 839-2111
CATALOG $4.

Rose Acres
6641 Crystal Blvd.
El Dorado, CA 95623
(916) 626-1722
SEND A SASE.

**Roses of Yesterday
and Today**
803 Browns Valley Rd.
Watsonville, CA 95076
(408) 724-3537 (phone)
(408) 724-1408 (fax)
CATALOG $3. SPECIALIZES IN OLD,
RARE AND UNUSUAL VARIETIES.

Royall River Roses
70 New Gloucester Rd.
North Yarmouth, ME 04097
(207) 829-5830 (phone)
(207) 829-6512 (fax)
CATALOG $3. SPECIALIZES IN OLD,
UNCOMMON AND HARDY ROSES.

**The Antique Rose
Emporium**
9300 Lueckemeyer Rd.
Brenham, TX 77833
(409) 836-9051 (phone)
(409) 836-0928 (fax)
100-PAGE COLOR CATALOG $5.

Wayside Gardens
1 Garden Lane
Hodges, SC 29695
(800) 845-1124
FREE CATALOG.

BIBLIOGRAPHY

INTERESTING INFORMATION ON ROSES is everywhere the reader turns to look. Unfortunately, much of it is useless to the northern rose grower bent on growing tender roses. The following sources offer valuable reading on a variety of rose-related subjects.

The Old Shrub Roses, Graham Stuart Thomas (London: J.M. Dent, 1985).
Shrub Roses of Today, Graham Stuart Thomas, (London: J.M. Dent, 1985).
Written by an acknowledged expert on shrub roses, these books are worth having if you are a garden book collector or really want to understand the shrub rose varieties. No color pictures, but the volumes are quite well written and contain more information than the average gardener wants or needs.

Hardy Roses, Robert Osborne (Vt.: Garden Way, 1991).
Osborne lists a variety of shrub roses that are quite hardy in northern gardens. Good color pictures complement the text.

Classic Roses, Peter Beales (N.Y.: Henry Holt & Co., 1985).
Recommended if you love huge colored pictures of dependable roses.

David Austin's English Roses, David Austin (London: Octopus, 1993).
The Austin, or English, roses are a wonderful form of rose when grown in northern conditions. Fragrant blossoms earn their way in my garden. This book describes most of the family and will give the reader a sense of which rose to put where in the perennial garden. If I could grow only one form of rose, it would be the English rose.

I HAVE ALSO HAUNTED BOOK SALES AND used book stores to find that interesting information is often buried under the piles of paperback mysteries in the back corner. It was in this way that I found:

Roses — Growing for Exhibiting, Harold Allen (Princeton: D. Van Nostrand Co., 1961).
Offers useful information on caring for summer roses with the idea of producing the most gorgeous blooms possible. You don't have to want to exhibit roses to get good ideas from these pages.

EVERY NOW AND THEN, YOU'LL COME across a copy of the *American Rose Annual* of the American Rose Society. One book is produced every year, and these make fascinating reading, especially the sections where members vote for their favorite or least favorite rose of the year. I recently picked up 20 consecutive years of these annuals for one dollar apiece. A true bargain.

IN THE 1930S, THERE WAS A SERIES OF books printed under the title *The Home Garden Handbooks* by Frederick F. Rockwell. Most can be found in garage sales or used book stores. The one on roses is full of useful, if a touch dated, advice.

PHOTOGRAPHY CREDITS

Richard W. Brown
Pages 17, 29, 42, 45, 50, 54, 56-57, 58-59, 75.

Derek Fell
Pages 3, 9, 12, 14, 28, 35, 36, 53, 61, 74,
78, 84, 86, 90, 100, 111, 113.

Douglas Green
Pages 46, 85.

Saxon Holt
Front cover and pages 10, 14-15, 16, 22, 24, 27,
30, 32, 38, 41, 43, 59, 62, 63,67, 68, 70, 72,
82, 83, 87, 101, 105, 107.

Index

Index